P9-BBT-735

Frances Tenenbaum, Series Editor

HOUGHTON MIFFLIN COMPANY
Boston • New York 2000

The Cutting Garden

Plants for gorgeous bouquets all year long

ROB PROCTOR

Copyright © 2000 by Houghton Mifflin Company
Text and photos copyright © 2000 by Rob Proctor

All rights reserved

For information about permission to reproduce selections from this book, write to Permissions, Houghton Mifflin Company, 215 Park Avenue South, New York, New York 10003.

Taylor's Guide and *Taylor's Weekend Gardening Guides* are registered trademarks of Houghton Mifflin Company.

Library of Congress Cataloging-in-Publication Data

Proctor, Rob.
The cutting garden / Rob Proctor.
p. cm. — (Taylor's weekend gardening guides)
Includes index.
ISBN 0-395-82945-3
1. Flower gardening. 2. Cut flowers. 3. Flowers. 4. Flower arrangement. I. Title. II. Series.
SB405.P885 2000
635.9'66—dc21 99-28990

Printed in the United States of America

WCT 10 9 8 7 6 5 4 3 2 1

Book design by Deborah Fillion
Cover photograph © by Rob Proctor

CONTENTS

INTRODUCTION 1

CHAPTER 1 — DESIGNING THE CUTTING GARDEN 7

CHAPTER 2 — PLANNING AND MAINTAINING THE CUTTING GARDEN 21

CHAPTER 3 — SPRING FLOWERS 31

CHAPTER 4 — SUMMER BOUNTY 49

CHAPTER 5 — AUTUMN GLORIES 83

CHAPTER 6 — CUTTING AND ARRANGING 101

CHAPTER 7 — ENDLESS SUMMER 107

INDEX 115

Few things are as beautiful as a bouquet of garden flowers. Among the most compelling reasons to garden is the joy of growing flowers for picking, in combinations that suit your tastes and change throughout the seasons. It takes only energy and inspiration to turn a neglected corner or boring stretch of lawn into a productive source of fresh flowers.

A cutting garden can be little more than a vegetable plot given over to rows of flowers, but it doesn't have to be; it can be beautiful in its own right, suiting the style of the owner and complementing the rest of the landscape and home.

Your own cutting garden offers far more than a florist ever could. The cut flower industry is driven by long-stemmed beauties that look great in tall buckets in the cooler or on the street corner. This severely limits the

A crescent arrangement of black-eyed Susans, gladiolus, garden phlox, zinnias, and marigolds turns a cutting garden into a landscape focal point.

selection. Height is not a primary consideration for the home gardener, who may find joy in a coffee mug of pansies on a desk, a tiny jar of lily-of-the-valley on the night stand, or a sugar bowl stuffed with spicy sweet peas on the breakfast table. Many gardeners also like floating a blossom or two in a pretty China dish or rose bowl.

In spring, there are bouquets of glory-of-the-snow, primroses, and hyacinths waiting outside to be picked. Daffodils and tulips come in waves (if you splurged last fall) and at a bargain price compared with the florist's. Sunny weather brings out perennials like peonies, iris, and columbine. Well-selected shrubs and trees provide a wealth of flowers for cutting as well—from forsythia, quince, and apple blossoms that can be forced to bloom ahead of schedule indoors, to lilacs, bridal veil, and mock orange. These extend the boundaries of the cutting garden to include the entire home landscape.

Even before the spring bulbs and early perennials finish, activity intensifies in the cutting garden as the gardener sows annuals and summer-flowering bulbs. The seeds of sunflowers, zinnias, and bachelor's buttons are easy to germinate, providing armloads of flowers for picking in a short time. Easy bulbs and bulbous plants include gladiolus, sweet-smelling acidanthera, liatris, and tuberoses. It's also time to sow everlasting flowers — annuals that can be cut and dried — such as strawflowers *(Helichrysum bracteatum),* globe amaranth *(Gomphrena globosa),* and annual ornamental grasses.

Gardeners can customize their freshly picked bouquets by selecting and growing plants in colors they most enjoy. Pastel lovers can concentrate on shades that complement their interior décor, while people who love bright colors can throw caution to the wind. Each bouquet presents the opportunity to create a personal expression from the bounty of the cutting garden.

Perennials that bloom over an extended period — Indian blanket *(Gaillardia aristata),* tickseed (*Coreopsis* spp.), and pincushion flowers (*Scabiosa* spp.) — carry through the summer heat in many areas of the country. As autumn arrives, the cutting garden continues to produce. Black-eyed Susans *(Rudbeckia hirta),* mums, and asters flower profusely. Pumpkins, squash, gourds, berries, pods, and autumn foliage add another dimension to homegrown arrangements, especially for Halloween and Thanksgiving displays. The autumn abundance may remind the gardener to plant both perennials and bulbs for next season.

In winter — surrounded by bouquets of everlastings — a gardener takes on the pleasant task of searching seed catalogs for new varieties for the coming year.

Plump 'Blue Jacket' hyacinths and brilliant 'Orange Sun' tulips make spring flower arrangements easy.

But even at this time of year for gardeners in cold climates, the cutting garden provides a source of intriguing material. Rose hips, winterberries, and desiccated seedpods add texture to arrangements with glossy holly, fragrant conifers, and sleek branches of red-twig dogwood.

An art degree isn't necessary to create beautiful homegrown arrangements, but some practical gardening knowledge is. Selecting the right site for your cutting garden is important. Evaluating and amending the soil is just as important. A few months in the garden will make you adept at sowing seeds, transplanting perennials, watering, fertilizing, and staking, but I'll give you some tips to help you get started. In addition, I'll also explain when and how to cut flowers and condition them for long-lasting arrangements.

In this book, I have highlighted classic annuals, bulbs, perennials, vines, and woody plants that perform admirably across much of the nation in a variety of conditions. I have avoided novelty hybrids or introductions that may become obsolete within a few years. Flowers that fare poorly in a vase aren't mentioned, but if you have a particular favorite, it's worth experimenting to see if you can make it last. Otherwise, be content to enjoy it outside.

Tickseed *(Coreopsis)*

The zigzag pattern on the petals of Gaillardia aristata *shows why it's commonly called Indian blanket; lime green flowering tobacco accompanies it in the cutting garden.*

CHAPTER 1

DESIGNING THE CUTTING GARDEN

A cutting garden can take many shapes. For gardeners with plenty of space, the ideal way to create a cutting garden may be to select a special spot and plan the garden there. For those of us for whom space is a more valuable commodity, it's a matter of finding a creative way to squeeze a cutting garden into the existing layout. There's always a way. Maybe the old vegetable garden needs a makeover (the joy of growing zucchini often pales over the years), or there's no need for the space once reserved for the kids' swing set and sand pile. Perhaps a tree has died and opened up a new area. Maybe you could put that neglected area by the garage to good use.

Most of us have more than we think if we dare to encroach upon the lawn. If I were looking for a site in my own yard, my immediate thoughts would go to what I grandly call the "croquet lawn," though in six seasons we've yet to play a single game there. I'd claim the middle of it for a cutting garden. (Since I already have several cutting areas in my overstuffed garden, my musings are hypothetical until I actually get out a shovel to attack the lawn.)

A crisp white picket fence encloses a cutting garden filled with bachelor buttons, purple coneflowers, cosmos, sunflowers, and silver artemisia.

Pick a sunny site. Not everyone has a site where the sun shines from dawn to dusk, but four or five hours ought to suffice for most sun lovers. Even a shadier spot can provide a wealth of flowers if you choose wisely and forgo the cosmos and sunflowers.

I've always thought that a proper cutting garden benefits from an enclosure of some sort. Many gardeners employ an enclosure for an herb or rose garden; a cutting garden can use one as well. A picket fence, a low stone wall, wattle fencing of woven willow, rustic cedar planks, or clipped hedges announce that some special sort of gardening is happening within. A fence of some sort also provides support for climbers as well as plants that often need staking such as dahlias or delphiniums. It's much easier to run some twine along the length of a fence to hold up these easily broken plants than to stake each one individually. Even a simple wire fence can be covered with a cloak of sweet peas or climbing roses, turning a utilitarian object into a thing of practical beauty. A fence may also keep out rabbits, deer, or other wildlife that would find the contents of a cutting garden tempting. Arbors and trellises add more opportunities to beautify the garden and grow climbing plants for cutting.

Inside the enclosure, there are a number of ways to proceed with the plan. It's practical and pleasing to divide a space into a pattern, with paths for walking and for working. A simple square, for example, may be easily divided into four equal parts with a walkway dividing them. Add a diamond in the center and the plan becomes more intricate. Play with half-circles and rectangles and suddenly you've created a parterre. I would certainly play with all this on paper before I started to lay it out in brick or stone. I used cedar fence pickets to work out the design in my own cutting garden, laying them out to show the beds and paths before I bricked the edges. Keep your beds small enough that you can reach into the center of the bed without stepping into it and compacting the soil.

Many gardeners make a parterre out of raised beds. This has a number of advantages, the main two being able to fill the beds with wonderful topsoil and ease of maintenance for those who dislike stooping and bending. Like ordinary beds, raised beds may be positioned in any pleasing manner, depending on the gardener's carpentry skills. Gardeners with heavy clay soils can use raised beds to provide their cutting beds with good topsoil without carting off the underlying clay. About eight inches of good topsoil in a raised bed is enough for most plants.

A raised bed provides armloads of feverfew, sweet Williams, daisies, and globe thistle for cutting.

Long-stemmed Shasta daisies are perennial favorites for arranging.

Facing page: Simple raised beds contain larkspur, cosmos, statice, and coreopsis.

A friend built simple raised beds, two by four feet, with two-foot pathways, arranged in a U-shape in her rectangular cutting garden. The center is left open for a bench and pots, while the simple wire fence enclosing the garden (to keep out bunnies) surrounds the beds with a living tapestry of morning glories, sweet peas, and scarlet runner beans. The arrangement is convenient and pleasing to the eye. There's something to be said for providing a focal point in a cutting garden, whether it's a statue, birdbath, or grouping of pots. There's even more to be said for providing a bench for buckets, baskets, and your own behind.

Then there's the matter of planting within the beds, no matter what shape they take. The practical gardener may opt for perfect rows. This is for the stake-

and-string set who enjoy planting seeds each spring in the tradition of Mr. MacGregor (Peter Rabbit's nemesis). They create furrows to catch water, space the seeds evenly, and mark each row with a tidy label. Veteran vegetable gardeners might choose this route.

I discovered rather late in my gardening career that I really dislike rows. I used to make perfect ones — as I was trained to do as a boy — but they brought out the worst in my personality. I fussed over them constantly, worrying about the spacing, transplanting where the neighborhood cats had scratched out the seedlings or the cutworms had gotten at the zinnias. It drove me nuts.

Now I plant everything in drifts and clumps. There's more room for creativity and failures don't show as badly — a gap in a row where a seed failed to germinate is much more noticeable than a plant missing from a drift or clump. It also allows me to incorporate flowers and foliage for cutting — annuals, perennials, biennials, bulbs, and even vegetables — in a looser, more workable framework. A patch of tulips can be overplanted with annuals as the tulip foliage fades; perennial baby's breath, just a few inches high when the daffodils bloom, takes over the space after the bulbs go dormant. Careful placement helps me have something for a bouquet throughout the growing season. Planting annuals amid bulb foliage helps to protect young transplants and soon hides the fading bulb foliage.

Having a cutting garden helps to expand what a gardener uses in indoor arrangements. I've gotten pretty wild lately. I'll use corn tassels, sprays of cherry tomatoes, branches of rose hips, and even roadside weeds. But I still love the traditional flowers. I can't resist making a bouquet of golden daffodils, plump peonies, luscious lilies, or bountiful black-eyed Susans. I never tire of these. By planning around these star performers, it's possible to create personalized bouquets. Although some flowers, like roses, are classics displayed by themselves, make sure there are companion flowers at every season to complement your favorite show stoppers. In spring, for example, I combine tulips or daffodils with flowering branches of forsythia, quince, or fruit trees. A vase of peonies looks even better with chartreuse lady's mantle *(Alchemilla vulgaris),* Spode blue peach-

Small beds surrounded by grass paths hold a wealth of cutting flowers: veronica, white yarrow, and daisies.

leaf bellflowers *(Campanula persicifolia),* or creamy white goatsbeard *(Aruncus dioicus).* The Asiatic lilies of June and July look great arranged with deep blue larkspur, simple white daisies, or lavender. And in late summer and autumn, a bouquet of black-eyed Susans is enhanced with stunning shiny seeds of blackberry lilies *(Belamcanda chinensis),* northern sea oats *(Chasmanthium latifolium),* and sprays of oregano.

Many gardeners have favorite colors that they use to enhance their home décor. I'm not very particular; in fact I'm nearly indiscriminate, but that doesn't mean that someone who loves blue and yellow together shouldn't plan their cutting garden to reflect that. From yellow daffodils, roses, lilies, and mums to blue ornamental onion *(Allium caeruleum),* delphinium, blue lace flower *(Trachymene caerulea),* sea holly *(Eryngium planum),* and globe thistle *(Echinops ritro),* they can always be assured of a supply of color-coordinated floral arrangements. People who live in houses full of pastel chintz shouldn't bother to plant red-hot-pokers or scarlet dahlias.

Sometimes we forget how foliage can play an important role in bouquets. Ornamental grasses, hostas, and many other plants we value in the garden for their attractive leaves add just as much to an arrangement. Silver foliage, such as that of dusty miller *(Senecio cineraria),* various artemisias (*Artemisia* spp.), and cotton lavender *(Santolina chamaecyparissus),* adds highlights to a bouquet. I think those silver or gray leaves bring out the best in pastel flowers. Chartreuse or golden foliage, such as that displayed by golden-leafed feverfew (*Tanacetum parthenium* 'Aureum'), golden hops vine (*Humulus lupus* 'Aureus'), or many hostas, really jazzes up an arrangement of bright-colored blossoms, especially hot pink and bright blue. Bronze foliage, cut from a purple-leafed smoke bush *(Cotinus coggygria),* sand cherry *(Prunus cistena),* bronze fennel (*Foeniculum vulgare* 'Purpureum'), Chinese basil *(Perilla frutescens),* or dark forms of New Zealand flax (*Phormium* spp.), creates a dramatic accent in a bouquet, especially paired with fiery orange or crimson.

Variegated leaves may also be employed to create a unique accompaniment to flowers. I especially like using variegated grasses or rushes with white or creamy yellow flowers. The leaves of streaked, striped, and emargined hostas (if the slugs haven't gotten to them) are lovely at the base of an arrangement to set off a cluster of white roses or lilies. There are hundreds of cultivars of popular flowers with variegated leaves, so often it's possible to get both blooms and striking

Ornamental grasses, such as maiden grass and striped Hakonechloa macra, *add lovely textures to bouquets and gardens.*

Vines for Cutting (Flowers, Foliage, or Seeds)

Bittersweet *(Celastrus orbiculatus)*
Pesky seeder and rampant grower, but the orange fruit makes good addition to fresh or dried arrangements. Be sure not to plant it yourself, though.

Chinese lantern *(Physalis alkekengi)*
Papery lanterns can be grown on wire or wooden support; charming in fresh or dry bouquets.

Clematis (*Clematis* spp.)
Condition in tepid water for a day before arranging to avoid wilting, or float in a bowl.

Climbing hydrangea *(Hydrangea petiolaris)*
Creamy white flower heads can be floated when fresh or may be dried.

Gourds (*Cucubita* spp.)
Allow to scramble on the ground or train onto a sturdy trellis.

Grape (*Vitex* spp.)
Enormous leaves and graceful tendrils are useful in big, ambitious arrangements.

Honeysuckle (*Lonicera* spp.)
Long sprays of white, pink, or coral red tubular flowers useful for trailing effect in bouquets. Avoid planting the invasive *L. japonica.*

Hops (*Humulus lupus*)
Leaves and fruit useful in fresh or dried bouquets; often used for swags and wreaths; the gold leaf form 'Aureus' and variegated Japanese 'Variegatus' are striking.

Hyacinth bean *(Dolichos lablab)*
Pretty pink pea flowers accented by bronzy leaves and purple pods later.

Ivy *(Hedera helix)*
Green or variegated leaves make long-lasting accompaniment to other flowers.

Jasmine (*Jasminum* spp.)
Add a fragrant spray to a bouquet to perfume an entire room.

Mina *(Mina lobata)*
Like very orderly sweet peas stacked geometrically on the stem; bottom flowers are orange-red and top ones are cream.

Passionflower (*Passiflora* spp.)
Dramatic scarlet, blue, or cream and purple flowers best viewed in a bowl.

Perennial pea *(Lathyrus latifolius)*
Hot pink or white peas lack fragrance but grow almost anywhere; pick long pieces of vine if desired.

Porcelain vine *(Ampelopsis brevipedunculata)*
Lovely blue-black berries pretty in wild arrangements; needs substantial support and room.

Silver-lace vine *(Polygonum aubertii)*
Tiny white flowers are produced in profusion; good for weaving through big bouquets.

Sweet pea *(Lathyrus odoratus)*
Feed and water religiously for best results; great on wire fencing or trellis.

Trumpet vine *(Campsis radicans)*
Scarlet or yellow tubular flowers have high impact; needs strong support and discipline.

Virginia creeper *(Parthenosissus tricuspidata)*
Crimson fall foliage recommends it for fiery accent; condition in tepid water immediately after cutting.

A clematis-clad arbor announces the entrance to a cutting garden stuffed with delphinium, lilies, and baby's breath; the huge clematis flowers are lovely floated in a bowl.

leaves on the same plant. Variegated varieties of shrubs such as euonymus, holly, and privet make splendid "fillers" for an otherwise pedestrian bouquet.

Not every plant will fit into the enclosure labeled as a cutting garden. Look at the entire home landscape for inspiration. All sorts of trees, shrubs, and vines offer distinctive foliage at different times of the year, especially in autumn. Vines, in particular, grown on trelliswork, fences, or arbors that encircle a cottage garden, provide lovely flowers, seeds, and foliage. Many woody plants display interesting bark and branches. Pods, berries, and fruit expand the options for the home flower arranger even further.

If space is limited, you don't need a specific cutting garden to pick plenty of flowers for your home. By planting prolific bloomers throughout your landscape, such as in perennial borders and annual flower beds, you'll still have many flowers from which to select. Though it's tempting to plant only annuals that keep producing abundantly over an extended period, don't discount the charms of the many plants — bulbs, perennials, vines, shrubs, and trees — that bloom only once a year. A peony is so spectacular and a tulip so delightful that most flower arrangers can't do without them, even though they're just a once-a-year experience. A few perennials, especially those from the daisy family, bloom almost as abundantly as annuals do. And hybrid tea and shrub roses often provide a constant supply of flowers.

Many gardeners prefer to combine flowers for cutting with vegetables. This time-honored tradition makes sense, as a vegetable garden keeps changing as crops are planted and harvested. Many annuals may be directly seeded in the ground at the same time vegetables are planted. And just as there are cool-season vegetable crops such as peas, radishes, and spinach, there are cool-season annuals like pot marigold *(Calendula officinalis)* and stock *(Matthiola incana).* When the weather heats up, the early crops of vegetables and flowers fizzle. They can be pulled up and composted, making room for warm-season vegetables such as beans, corn, and squash, as well as heat-loving annual flowers such as zinnias, marigolds, and sunflowers.

Goatsbeard *(Aruncus)*

Orange pot marigolds (Calendula officinalis) *and red Shirley poppies sow themselves from year to year if a few plants are left to go to seed.*

Chapter 2

Planning and Maintaining the Cutting Garden

Before you can cut flowers, you've got to grow them. Not everyone can grow everything. Climate often makes some choices for us. Space (or lack of it) forces us to make more choices. But a cutting garden opens the door to experimenting with and growing flowers that aren't always available from the florist.

Plants that aren't cut out for my climate announce it quite clearly and end their days in the compost pile. There's no shame in admitting that you can't grow something, and each failure teaches a lesson. Every new season brings the opportunity to experiment. There are literally thousands of plants that grow successfully in any given region, so why waste time and energy spraying and worrying over those that aren't suited to your environment?

There's no magic that ensures a floriferous garden: it's just good, basic gardening. Beginning gardeners often succeed with annuals and a few basic perennials. As their skill and confidence grow, they begin to scour seed and nursery catalogs and get to know the employees at every nursery in town.

Orange zinnias consort handsomely with fountain grass.

Success begins with evaluating your site for what it will grow best. A sunny site offers a few more options than a shady one, but there's no need to be daunted by shade. A great number of perennials, annuals, bulbs, vines, and shrubs thrive in partial shade. Conversely, these shade lovers won't appreciate a hot, sunny position. There are always tradeoffs.

Soil is an important consideration in growing anything. A deep, sandy loam is ideal for a great many plants, but many of us don't have it. Soil amendment becomes necessary for heavy clay soil or a very sandy one. Organic matter — in the form of compost, well-rotted manure, or leaf mold — is usually the answer for either one. Organic matter in the soil helps maintain good drainage in clay soils, aids in water retention in sandy ones, and helps keep plant nutrients available in both. Consult your local extension agent or master gardener program for the best methods in your area to amend your soil to grow a broader variety of plants. There are no generalizations that apply to all areas. Some people bring in topsoil when there seems to be little hope of turning a rock pile or brickyard into a garden. Raised beds are a great benefit to many gardeners, although they are difficult to keep moist in arid and semiarid areas.

It's just as difficult to generalize about water and fertilizer. Where rainfall is ordinarily plentiful, there's usually little concern about supplemental irrigation. Even so, everyone goes through a drought sooner or later. And in many regions, summer irrigation is a necessity. Some gardeners prefer to use the tried-and-true hose and sprinkler system. Others like underground pop-up sprinkler systems; still others utilize drip irrigation. There are advantages and disadvantages to every method. Time, money, and experience will help you decide. I use a combination of "leaky" hoses (flexible, perforated rubber hoses that stay permanently in place and water slowly by the drip method) as well as overhead watering with a hose and sprinkler. I decide when to turn them on. Sometimes I wish for a high-tech automatic system, but a fully automated system doesn't account for temperature and recent rainfall, and can end up overwatering the plants. Despite the work, I prefer to irrigate only when my plants really need it.

Many people use too much fertilizer. The worst-case scenario is to actually "burn" plants with an excess of nitrogen (you often see lawns that have burned stripes from too much nitrogen). I'm also concerned about groundwater contamination from the overuse of fertilizer. Plants that are growing well don't need help from a bag. On the other hand, compost provides essential elements for

plant growth and blossoming. I top-dress my beds with compost several times a year and incorporate more when planting, digging, and transplanting.

A little commercial fertilizer can be useful at times; young annuals may benefit from some nitrogen, and potassium can promote better blossoming. Commercial fertilizers, both organic and inorganic types, are made up of three principal components, often with trace elements added. The three components are generally denoted by the chemist's shorthand — N for nitrogen, P for phosphorous, and K for potassium. Nitrogen is actually not very useful in the production of flowers: too much promotes vigorous foliage but few flowers (that's why most lawn fertilizers have very high nitrogen content). Roses often require chemical boosts; check with local experts to see which supplemental fertilizers they require in your area. I shy away from fertilizing perennials at any time, since I think this promotes lank, soft growth and floppy stems. I am in favor of a good shot of a well-balanced (say 20-20-20) water-soluble fertilizer to help get new annual transplants off to a good start.

I also don't promote any pesticides or fungicides stronger than insecticidal soap, dormant oil sprays, pyrethrum, or sulfur. Some gardeners rely on natural home brews of garlic, peppers, and the like. I rarely use anything at all; my allies are the birds and good insects that thrive in my pesticide-free garden.

I grow a great many plants, mainly annuals and perennials, from seed. Some I sow directly in the garden, while others are grown under lights in my basement. Cool-season annuals can be sown directly in the soil in either autumn or late winter in most areas. Rough up the soil with a rake or cultivator and sow the seed according to packet directions. Generally, very fine seed is sown very shallowly (with just a fine layer of soil covering it), and larger seed is poked further down. I pat fine seed down with my hands to ensure contact is made (and that it doesn't blow away). Some people use a board to do this.

Warm-season annuals such as zinnias and marigolds are sown the same way, but these tropical plants shouldn't go out until the soil temperature suits them (usually when night temperatures stay above 50°F). This varies from region to region, of course. All seeds need to be kept moist but not soggy during the germination period. Drying out at this critical stage means crop failure. Some gardeners keep the soil moist with a covering of fabric row cover, cheesecloth, or other lightweight fabric that both light and water can penetrate.

It's easy to grow annuals from seed indoors. It doesn't require a greenhouse,

just a sunny window or heated porch. I use my basement, employing inexpensive shop lights from the hardware store set on tables made from saw horses and plywood. The lights are fitted with regular inexpensive fluorescent bulbs (I have experimented with more expensive "grow lights" but didn't find they affected my seedlings one way or the other).

I sow the seeds directly in recycled six-packs set in plastic flats with convenient plastic domes. A sterile seed-starting soil mixture (available from your garden center) is essential to keep newly sprouted plants from contracting fungus diseases. Sow the seeds according to the directions on the seed packet, which also usually tell you how many weeks before your last frost to sow. Subtract backward from the last average frost-free date in your region to determine when it's best to sow. Contact your county extension agent or local botanical gardens if you're not sure.

After sowing, water the tray of six-packs from the bottom (to avoid washing out the seeds), cover with a clear plastic dome or plastic wrap, and place under lights or in the windowsill. Plants grown in the window or porch often benefit from supplemental artificial lighting. I place my flats of six-packs directly below the fluorescent lights, which are hung from my basement ceiling on chains so they can be raised as the plants grow. It's ideal to keep the plants just an inch or two below but not touching the tubes. Remove the plastic domes as the seeds germinate. I usually plant three or four seeds in each cell. Thin to one as they come up. Feed lightly with a weak solution of 20-20-20 fertilizer in water every few days. Continue to water from the bottom to allow the roots to soak up water without washing soil away. Don't keep temperatures too high or the plants will grow too quickly and become spindly. Between 60° and 70°F by day and slightly cooler at night is ideal for most annuals. My basement is on the dry side, so I spray the foliage several times a day with water from a spray bottle.

When the young plants have reached transplanting stage and the weather has moderated, harden off the seedlings by moving them outside. The young leaves are extremely sensitive to sunlight (like your own skin in spring) and must be exposed gradually. Place them in dappled shade for the first few days, gradually moving them into a sunnier position. If you don't have a tree beneath which to shelter your seedlings, you'll need to keep on your toes, shuttling the flats in and out of the sun. It usually takes 3 to 5 days to get the seedlings ready for transplanting to the garden.

Iceland poppies may wilt soon after cutting unless the base of their stems is seared with a match and plunged into cold water. Poppies usually perform best if the seeds are sown directly in the garden.

The pastel blossoms of Nicotiana *'Salmon Pink' are contrasted effectively by the bronze leaves of* Perilla frutescens.

For some annuals, consider buying six-packs at your local nursery. Seeds are less expensive than transplants, but consider how much space you have on your windowsills, under lights, or in your greenhouse before you decide to grow every annual from seed. There's little reason to grow common annuals such as flowering tobacco *(Nicotiana alata),* dusty miller, snapdragons, or marigolds from seed unless you want certain unusual colors. When you buy from a garden center, look for husky young plants that aren't tightly root-bound in their containers. Select for healthy green foliage and compact growth (and make a check on the undersides of the leaves for signs of pests such as whiteflies or aphids).

Don't worry if the plants have few or no flowers—you'll want to pinch them all off before planting anyway. Pinching off blossoms allows young plants to put all of their energy into setting their roots down in your garden soil. A few annuals benefit from pinching out the growth tips to make them bushier and more productive. Do this at planting time with snapdragons, spider flower *(Cleome hasslerana),* marigolds, asters, flowering tobacco, and balsam *(Impatiens balsamina).* This will encourage multiple branching rather than one spindly single stem.

When transplanting, squeeze the plant out of its cell gently. Hold the root ball—not the stem, which is easily damaged—and insert it into the hole. Firm it in gently so the roots make contact with the soil, making a slight depression around it to collect moisture. Water thoroughly and avoid letting it dry out until the roots are well established.

The best time for transplanting nursery-grown or homegrown seedlings varies. Cool-season annuals can withstand a few degrees of frost; warm-season annuals generally come from tropical or subtropical regions and shouldn't go outside until night temperatures have warmed to 50°F or better. Otherwise they will stunt. Any plant that comes from under glass at the garden center must be hardened off for a few days by gradually exposing it to full sun. Plants displayed outdoors at garden centers can be transplanted as soon as you get home.

Annuals Best Grown by Direct Seeding in Place

Larkspur *(Consolida ambigua)*
Shirley poppy *(Papaver rhoeas)*
Opium poppy *(Papaver somniferum)*
Cosmos *(Cosmos bipinnatus)*
Love-in-a-mist *(Nigella damascena)*
Bachelor's buttons *(Centaurea cyanus)*
Annual baby's breath *(Gypsophila elegans)*

Perennials can be planted at most any time but are commonly set out in spring or fall in most parts of the country. Division is customarily done at the same times to increase stock and invigorate the plant, usually after three or four years. Some plants, such as sea holly (*Eryngium* spp.), delphinium, and gas plant *(Dictamnus albus),* almost never need to be divided or can't be divided successfully because of their taproot structure. These perennials may be propagated by seed or cuttings.

Whether a plant needs to be staked is up to the gardener and the growing conditions. In windy areas, staking is vital for flowers that are easily brought down by gusts. There are many methods of staking. Cages and hoops encircle a plant and keep it from flopping. Some gardeners create their own plant supports by weaving together twigs and brush or by running string or twine between stakes that encircle a plant. You can also make frames of chicken wire and suspend them horizontally off the ground, allowing plant stems to grow through the wire. Bamboo and wooden stakes may be used for tall flowers like dahlias and delphiniums. The trick is to secure the stake in the ground early in the season. Tether the plant to the stake as it grows, rather than trying to lash it up after it has already flopped to the ground. Many gardeners prefer soft cloth ties (such as strips of old pantyhose) for tying plants to stakes because they don't injure the stems. Whatever you use — twine and yarn are also good choices — make a loop around the stake, tie it, then loop around the stem of the plant and then tie that. This double loop system is not only more graceful but keeps the plant stem straight and secure.

Spider flower *(Cleome)*

An inconspicuous hoop helps to keep flowers that are easily damaged by wind, such as delphinium, secure.

Chapter 3
Spring Flowers

A spring bouquet, at least for gardeners who've endured a cold winter, is a touch of heaven. We might pick a few of the first minor bulbs, such as snowdrops, glory-of-the-snow, and squills, or a stem of dusky plum hellebores as they bloom. As the buds swell on the shrubs and trees, it's easy to cut a few branches (the fruit trees do need a bit of pruning). I mash the bottom few inches of each branch with a hammer to help them absorb water, stick them in a deep bucket, and keep them in a cool, dark place in the basement for a few days. Some people use an unheated garage or spare bedroom. They quickly burst into bloom.

The fragrance of the blossoms of peach, plum, apple, crabapple, pear, and cherry is delightful. Quince, witch hazel, pussy willow, and forsythia can also be forced into bloom. It's worth trying most any flowering tree or shrub; wait for the buds to swell before cutting and bringing the branches indoors. Some gardeners even like to cut the branches of deciduous trees such as maple, ash, or aspen for the fresh green leaves. Curly willow provides architectural drama to a bouquet. Filberts and birch are valued for their drooping catkins.

It's worth stocking up on favorite colors of bulbs, such as these plum purple 'Hans Anrud' tulips, for unique bouquets.

TREE AND SHRUB BRANCHES

Symbols (❀) indicate species whose blooms are easily forced.

- **Almond** ❀ *(Prunus dulcis)*
  Lightly scented white or pink blossoms; some forms have double flowers.

- **Apple** ❀ *(Malus pumila)*
  Sweet fragrance of single pale pink flowers is delightful.

- **Apricot** ❀ *(Prunus armeniaca)*
  White, softly scented single blossoms.

- **Aspen** *(Populus tremula)*
  Only male trees have showy pale yellow catkins, but "cotton" may be annoying to tidy housekeepers.

- **Birch** (*Betula* spp.)
  Branches with drooping catkins make great accompaniment for arrangements of spring-flowering bulbs.

- **Cherry** ❀ (*Prunus* spp.)
  Slightly fragrant, single or double flowers in white or pink, depending on the variety.

- **Citrus** (*Citrus* spp.)
  Powerfully fragrant flowers are a wonderful addition to bouquets.

- **Curly willow** (*Salix sachalinensis* 'Sekka')
  Twisting branch structure adds instant architecture to a bouquet.

- **Daphne** (*Daphne* spp.)
  Late winter or spring flowers of white or pale pink carry intoxicating scent.

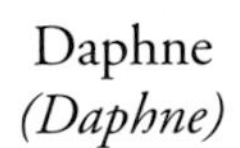
Daphne
(Daphne)

- **Flowering quince** ❀ (*Chaenomeles* spp.)
  Vibrant red, apricot pink, or white flowers appear before the leaves.

Branches cut from winter-flowering witch hazel are a welcome indoor decoration.

- **Forsythia** ❀ (*Forsythia* spp.)
The quintessential shrub for early forcing; easy and rewarding.

- **Harry Lauder's walking stick**
(*Corylus avellana* 'Contorta')
The curly branches make exciting bouquets and may be dried and reused.

- **Lilac** (*Syringa* spp.)
A bit tricky to force but great for cutting when in full bloom; single or double flowers in purple, white, pink, and classic lavender-blue.

Magnolia
(Magnolia)

- **Magnolia** (*Magnolia* spp.)
Lovely in flower, but leaves are also valuable for wreaths and other arrangements.

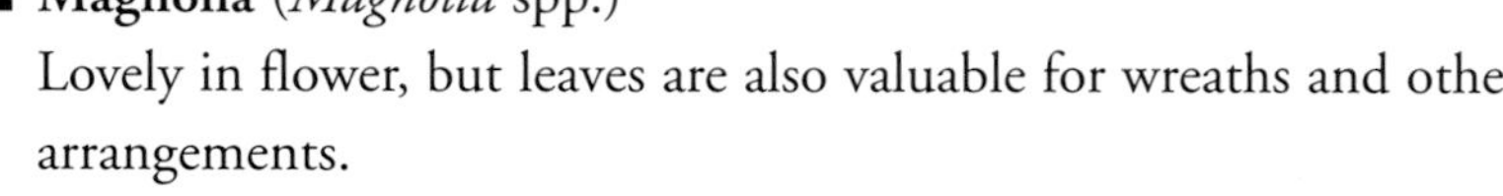

- **Peach** ❀ *(Prunus persica)*
Thick clusters of single white, slightly fragrant flowers.

- **Pear** ❀ (*Pyrus* spp.)
Double or single flowers, depending on variety, with faint fragrance.

- **Plum** ❀ (*Prunus* spp.)
Single flowers in pink or white; fragrance depends on variety.

- **Pussy willow** ❀ *(Salix chaenomeloides)*
Always charming in bouquets or displayed by themselves; easy to dry but somewhat fragile.

Redbud
(Cercis)

- **Redbud** ❀ (*Cercis* spp.)
Hot pink flowers are a perennial favorite and are great with spring bulbs.

- **Witch hazel** ❀ (*Hamamelis* spp.)
Winter-flowering species are wonderful to bring indoors; slight fragrance on cream or pale yellow tiny flowers.

The pendent sprays of Pieris japonica *hang above charming 'Thalia' daffodils.*

SPRING-FLOWERING BULBS

I always pat myself on the back when hyacinths, daffodils, and tulips start to bloom—especially if I took advantage of late autumn sales. Planting bulbs isn't my favorite garden chore. It's often cold and windy, and usually I've waited until a major storm is predicted for that evening. But the results are worth the trouble the following spring.

Many gardeners feel a twinge of guilt if they pick spring bulbs from their borders, but they're fair game in the cutting garden. Cut only the stems and leave the foliage intact to mature and replenish the bulb for the next year. By

selecting the right varieties for your area, you can almost be assured of a repeat crop of blossoms the next season and beyond. Daffodils are generally reliable, but most hyacinths decline a bit over time. Many tulips don't repeat well either. Fertilize the leaves as soon as they emerge and continue to feed them every week or so until they turn yellow. Don't remove them until they have withered. I prefer a fertilizer high in potash that is especially formulated for bulbs or — surprisingly — tomatoes. Many people advocate planting tulip bulbs deep (at least 8 inches), thinking that this makes them more likely to come back. I think this is a myth. The correct depth for hybrid tulips is 5 or 6 inches deep, depending on soil (deeper in sandy soil, more shallow in clay). We'll discuss tulips that repeat best below.

Turning the pages of a bulb specialist catalog can be confusing. Which daffodils are best? To have blooms for cutting over an extended period, order a dozen or so of many different varieties. Smaller, early-blooming daffodils like yellow 'Tête-à-tête' and ivory 'Jenny' are among the first to bloom. Planting generous drifts ensures that there will be plenty for picking. Miniatures may be small, but they're big on charm. Tiny yellow 'Sundial', white and yellow 'Minnow', and sulfur yellow with white 'Pipit' are irresistible.

For most of us, the classic yellow daffodils such as 'Carlton' or 'King Alfred' make the quintessential spring bouquet. There's no such thing as too many. Cut when they first open, daffodils may last four or five days inside, depending on the temperature and humidity (hot, dry air hastens the demise of any cut flower). I like to have plenty of yellow daffodils at my disposal. I also enjoy white daffodils such as 'Ice Follies' or 'Mount Hood', as well as the so-called pink varieties like 'Salome' or 'Accent' that feature a pink trumpet surrounded by white petals, even if the pink is more of a salmon shade. Varieties with orange cups set against yellow petals, such as 'Scarlet O'Hara', 'Orange Progress', or 'Ceylon' are eye-catching.

For variety, I enjoy the clustered types with several smaller blossoms on each stem, such as pure white 'Thalia' or yellow and white 'Silver Chimes'. My favorite is 'Geranium', an oddly named variety with creamy white petals surrounding a short orange cup. Double daffodils like 'Golden Ducat' or yellow and white 'White Lion' delight some arrangers, though I find the heavy heads are easily broken in a spring shower. 'Rip van Winkle' is beyond double — it looks more like a dandelion than a narcissus, but this ancient variety is a strong grower. The

Lily-form tulips offer straight, long stems, elegant flower shapes, and lovely colors for bouquets.

butterfly or split-cup daffodils display an unusual structure where the central trumpet or cup has been turned into an overlay of extra petals. They don't stick around in my garden for long, so I plant a few dozen yellow and white 'Cassata' or salmon pink and white 'Palmares' every few years.

One of my very favorites is the classic poet's daffodil, characterized by white petals, a short cup rimmed in red, and a green center. One variety is known as 'Pheasant's Eye' for this unique coloration. I like this elegant, unusual flower (another similar cultivar is 'Actea') and find myself ordering more every autumn, perhaps because it's one of the last daffodils to bloom (which means it rarely

gets buried by a late snowstorm). It also persists and multiplies. I really appreciate that in a bulb.

Some tulip varieties are known for their staying power. Darwin hybrids, such as red 'Apledoorn', 'Yellow Apledoorn', deep pink 'Elizabeth Arden', and pale yellow 'Jewel of Spring' may last for decades in some gardens. Lily-form tulips, featuring graceful flowers with flaring, pointed petals, have also earned a reputation for being good repeaters. My personal favorites include yellow 'West Point', pink 'Mariette', orange 'Ballerina', white 'Triumphator', and cream and pink 'Elegant Lady'.

If you've gotten a super deal on tulips, such as a mixture of unlabeled varieties, it's possible to simply treat them as annuals. Cut the flowers and compost the bulbs. There's no waiting for the foliage to go through its horrid demise. Southern and West Coast gardeners, who live where winter temperatures rarely drop low enough to fulfill tulips' chilling requirement to bloom after the first season, typically treat them as annuals. (They need to refrigerate the bulbs for six weeks to provide an artificial winter before planting.) Even where winter temperatures are sufficiently low to suit tulips' chilling requirements, there's no reason not to treat some varieties (ones that repeat badly) as annuals. These include the flashy parrot types, cottage, single late, and most doubles (with the exception of the pretty pink 'Angelique'). I indulge myself every few years by planting a generous quantity of some classic tulips such as 'Apricot Beauty', plum purple 'Attila', and 'Queen of the Night', which blooms in an unusual shade of maroon bordering on black. None of these three favorites has any intention of putting down permanent roots in my garden, but the flowers are so lovely for bouquets that I enjoy them while they last and pull up and compost the bulbs after flowering.

Other spring-flowering bulbs that deserve space in a cottage garden are the camassias and the summer snowflake (*Leucojum vernum* usually blooms in spring), both of which prosper in damp soil. Also consider wood hyacinths *(Hyacinthoides hispanica),* lily-of-the-valley *(Convallaria majalis),* brodiaea *(Triteleia laxa),* Persian bells *(Fritillaria persica),* and alliums such as yellow *Allium moly* and pink *A. ostrowskianum.* Solomon's seal *(Polygonatum odoratum)* has tiny pendent white bells spaced along its arching stem. Though no rival for flashier tulips or daffodils, it adds graceful architecture to an arrangement. The variegated form is equally charming. As spring turns to summer, depend-

Shady areas are no problem for wood hyacinth (Hyacinthoides hispanica), *which displays its Spode blue bells in spring.*

Spring Bulbs for Cutting

Brodiaea *(Triteleia laxa)*
Funnel-shaped purple-blue flowers are borne on stiff, bare stems up to a foot long.

Camassia *(Camassia leichtlinii, C. quamash)*
Good long stems make these spikes of white or lavender-blue starry flowers easy to arrange.

Daffodil (*Narcissus* spp.)
Many colors and forms; condition in water by themselves to remove juices that adversely affect other cut flowers by changing water at least twice before arranging.

Glory-of-the-snow *(Chionodoxa luciliae)*
Pink or pale blue sprays of starry flowers; they last longer in cool rooms and are best for smaller bouquets.

Grape hyacinth *(Muscari armeniacum)*
Musky scent of spikes of blue bubble-like flowers chases away winter blues.

Hyacinth (*Hyacinthus* spp.)
The piercing sweet scent of blue, white, purple, pink, yellow, salmon, or raspberry red flowers is the ideal tonic for winter-weary gardeners.

Iris. Dutch iris *(Iris × hollandica),* with blue, yellow, or white flowers on long stems are favorites. **Spanish iris** *(I. xiphioides),* heavily veined petals in dusky shades of purple, blue, and brown, like Gothic versions of Dutch iris.

Bearded iris *(I. × germanica),* in a rainbow of colors with huge ruffled blooms that last best in cool conditions. **Siberian iris** *(I. sibirica),* mainly shades of blue and purple or white on very long stems. **Spuria iris** *(I. spuria),* yellow, purple, blue, or white blossoms much like Siberians but even taller.

Lily-of-the-valley *(Convallaria majalis)*
Graceful arched stems hold pendent white cups with delicious scent.

Ornamental onion *(Allium moly, A. ostrowskianum)*
Yellow *A. moly* has starry clusters on 8-inch stems and may be grown in partial shade; pink *A. ostrowskianum* has clusters of pink bells on 6-inch stems.

Persian bells *(Fritillaria persica)*
Long, stout stems support dusky maroon bells; avoid cutting foliage to allow bulb to reenergize for next season.

Snowdrops *(Galanthus nivalis)*
Charming pendent white flowers for small desktop bouquets.

Solomon's seal *(Polygonatum odoratum)*
The small white drooping bells aren't very showy by themselves, but the long arching stems have great architectural interest in spring bouquets.

Squill *(Scilla sibirica)*
True blue early charmers for teacups and ink bottles.

Summer snowflake *(Leucojum vernum)*
Long, leafless stems with clusters of pendent white bells on top; highly ornamental with daffodils or tulips.

Tulip (*Tulipa* spp.)
Carefully make an inch-long slit on stem just below flower to keep it from bending toward light source, or just let tulips do their dance.

Wood hyacinth *(Hyacinthoides hispanica)*
Pink, blue, or white flowers resemble hyacinths but may be grown in shade; ideal for small arrangements.

ing on where you live, Dutch and Spanish iris bloom, followed by bearded, Siberian, and spuria iris (the latter two grow from rhizomes but are often grouped with other bulbous plants). These are floral knockouts and last well as cut flowers.

Loads of lily-form and double 'Angelique' tulips ensure plenty of spring bouquets from this cutting garden; perennials will take over as they expand and the tulips fade.

Gardeners in the South and on the West Coast often grow winter- and spring-flowering bulbs that aren't hardy in other regions. Some of these make excellent cut flowers, such as crinum lily, spider lily, harlequin flower, amaryllis, freesia, calla lily, baboon flower, Persian buttercup or turban flower, anemone, flame flower, chasmanthe, and nerine. Many of these bulbs grow and flower in response to autumn and winter moisture (which means supplemental moisture may be necessary during dry years) and go dormant or cease flowering during the heat and drought of summer.

Spring Bulbs for the West Coast or South

Amaryllis *(Hippeastrum × hybridum)*
Most often grown as a potted plant, but also makes a dramatic cut flower.

Anemone *(Anemone coronaria)*
Black center stamens accent purple, red, white, or lavender petals surrounded by collar of green ferny foliage; good stiff stems.

Baboon flower *(Babiana stricta)*
Pretty upfacing cups of mainly purple, lavender, and wine red.

Calla lily *(Zantedeschia aethiopica)*
A flower arranger's best friend; even a single stem is exquisite.

Chasmanthe (*Chasmanthe* spp.)
Showy clusters of yellow or orange tubular blossoms atop long stems perfect for big bouquets.

Crinum lily *(Crinum × powelli)*
Pink or white trumpets on long, hollow stems like amaryllis.

Flame flower *(Tritonia crocata)*
Copper pink, salmon, orange, or white flowers are lovely open stars on long stems.

Freesia *(Freesia × hybrida)*
The puffy trumpets in lavender, pink, red, yellow, or white are carried on stiff stems for easy arranging; their scent is heavenly.

Harlequin flower *(Sparaxis tricolor)*
Yellow, orange, or cream flowers open wide to reveal contrasting etching in black, brown, or olive; wiry stems.

Nerine bowdenii
Graceful bright pink trumpets in clusters on straight, stiff stems; very long lasting.

Persian buttercup or **turban flower** *(Ranunculus asiaticus)*
Bright, multipetaled flowers on strong, leafless stems.

Spider lily *(Lycoris radiata)*
Showy trumpets in red, gold, or pink with spidery stamens; long straight stems for easy arranging.

Ranunculus asiaticus, *sometimes called Persian buttercups, appear to be fashioned from brilliantly colored tissue paper.*

COOL-SEASON ANNUALS

Early-blooming annuals make welcome additions to the first bouquets of spring. In areas with mild winters, a great variety of annuals thrive in cool temperatures and can even tolerate a light frost. Sow them in autumn or transplant them from nursery-grown stock in autumn to bloom in winter and spring. These include poor man's orchid, stock, dusty miller, pansies, nemesia, pot marigold, and annual dianthus.

Northern gardeners can start these and other cool-season annuals early indoors to push their bloom schedule ahead to accompany the bulbs, or purchase

Cool-season Annuals for Cutting

Dusty miller *(Senecio cineraria)*
Best from nursery transplants; silver foliage makes ideal companions for pastel flower bouquets.

English daisy *(Bellis perennis)*
Best from fall or winter transplants; pick tiny white, pink, or red daisies like pansies.

Flowering tobacco *(Nicotiana alata)*
Easy from seed, but most gardeners prefer transplants because seed is almost microscopic; chartreuse flowers are especially pretty fillers in bright bouquets.

Forget-me-not *(Myosotis sylvatica)*
Plant transplants in late summer or fall for a profusion of late winter and spring blue flowers; leave some to self-sow.

Iceland poppy *(Papaver nudicaule)*
Stained-glass colors of red, orange, yellow, peach, and white; let some self-sow.

Nemesia *(Nemesia strumosa)*
Easy from seed and not commonly found in nurseries; flowers look a little like small snapdragons and come in beautiful mixed colors.

Ornamental kale *(Brassica oleracea)*
Usually transplanted in autumn; pick a few leaves or the whole head for stunning foliage effect.

Pansy *(Viola wittrockiana)*
Keep picked throughout fall, winter, and spring but replace when hot weather prevails.

nursery plants for transplanting. Most can safely be set out in the garden when night temperatures don't dip much below freezing. The return of hot days puts an end to their flowering, at which point they may be pulled out and replaced with warm-season annuals.

Although most of the annuals on this list transplant easily, poppies and sweet peas usually perform best if the seeds are sown directly in the garden. Some annuals, such as snapdragons, dusty miller, pansies, and ornamental kale, are so readily available that most people prefer to buy them as husky young plants ready for the garden.

Poor man's orchid *(Schizanthus wisetonensis)*
Big clusters of small, orchidlike blossoms; best from nursery-grown stock.

Pot marigold *(Calendula officinalis)*
Easy and productive from seed; select tallest strains for best cutting.

Rocky Mountain garland *(Clarkia elegans)*
Double flowers are most often sold, but the singles have more wildflower charm.

Satin flower *(Godetia amoena)*
Vivid, poppylike blossoms in cherry red, pink, salmon, or white.

Shirley poppy *(Papaver rhoeas)*
A paint box of many colors would be needed to paint these; leave some seed heads to self-sow for next year.

Snapdragon *(Antirrhinum majus)*
Easily grown from seed, but most gardeners prefer nursery-grown transplants; select mixed or single colors.

Stock *(Matthiola incana)*
Easy from seed, but most gardeners prefer large nursery transplants.

Sweet pea *(Lathyrus odoratus)*
Old favorites in myriad colors; antique strains often exhibit best heat resistance as well as strongest scents.

Wallflower *(Cheiranthus cheiri)*
Best grown from transplants from garden centers in late summer or autumn; useful columns for cutting of red, gold, purple, orange, or burnt orange flowers.

No sunny spot for a cutting garden? Leopard's bane (Doronicum caucasicum) *displays its golden blossoms in shade early in the season.*

EARLY PERENNIALS

Early-blooming perennials for mixed bouquets include the yellow daisies of leopard's bane *(Doronicum caucasicum),* pink *Bergenia cordifolia* (with waxy, broad leaves that often have tints of beet red), the dangling pink, blue, or white bells of lungwort (*Pulmonaria* spp.), bleeding-heart *(Dicentra spectabilis),* basket-of-gold *(Aurinia saxitilis),* Lenten rose (*Helleborus* spp.), and primroses (*Primula* spp.). The candelabra primroses, with tiers of flowers in shades of red, yellow, orange, and pink, are the longest-stemmed primroses — making them ideal for cutting — but they thrive only in moist, even boggy soil. Hybrid polyantha primroses come in dazzling colors, but I'm much fonder of the hum-

A cutting garden can provide fresh flowers in all seasons, even in late winter when Lenten rose (Helleborus orientalis) *blooms.*

ble yellow English primrose *(Primula veris),* and it performs more faithfully in my garden in dappled shade. In fact, many of the early perennials, such as leopard's bane, bleeding-heart, and bergenia — not to mention almost all of the bulbs — may be grown in a partially shaded cutting garden. This is especially advantageous for people who garden beneath a canopy of deciduous trees. Spring-flowering bulbs and early perennials leaf out and bloom early, before most of the trees. They take advantage of the bright spring sun and, in the case of the bulbs, store energy for the next season and then go dormant as summer arrives.

CHAPTER 4
SUMMER BOUNTY

The cutting garden comes into its own in summer. It teems with annuals, perennials, roses, bulbs, and — most of all — annuals.

Annuals are among the easiest and most productive inhabitants of any cutting garden. Some can be grown from seed sown directly in the ground in spring, while others flower sooner if you buy transplants from the nursery or garden center. Of course you can buy any of these if you didn't have the time, the equipment (lights or a bright window), or the interest to grow plants from seed. Easy, direct-sown annuals include cosmos, sunflowers, balsam *(Impatiens balsamina),* sweet pea, larkspur, love-in-a-mist *(Nigella damascena),* and Shirley poppy. Conveniently transplanted annuals include annual black-eyed Susan, mealy-cup sage *(Salvia farinacea),* zinnia, annual pincushion flower, blue lace flower *(Trachymene caerulea), Ageratum houstonianum* 'Cut Wonder', tall verbena *(Verbena patagonica),* coleus, snapdragon, and flowering tobacco, including tall, fragrant white woodland tobacco *(Nicotiana sylvestris).*

Summer warmth brings on bright annuals for cutting: mealy-cup sage (Salvia farinacea), *lantana, and classic zinnia* (Zinnia angustifolia).

The classic 'California Giant' zinnias are still among the best for cutting.

Zinnias are on the comeback. Many gardeners have discovered that they're one of the best annuals for any cutting garden, requiring only regular moisture to produce a bumper crop. (Mildew sometimes affects the foliage, but it's easily stripped off before arranging.) These workhorses of the cutting garden are classified into several groups for the shape of their flowers. Dahlia-flowered types feature closely layered petals rounded at the ends. Cactus-flowered zinnias have pointed petals on shaggy heads (and like the cactus-flowered dahlias, don't look a thing like any cactus flower I've ever come across). The daisy-flowered types are single and look a bit more like the type of flower that a girl could use for the "He loves me; he loves me not" game.

For cutting, the wise selections among these groups are the taller sorts, such as the tried-and-true 'California Giant' strain, the better to have longer stems to arrange with. In addition, selections from the species *Zinnia angustifolia,* often called classic zinnia, have become quite popular. These are not like the tall, stiff varieties we usually associate with zinnias, but branch like a signet marigold and produce myriad smaller flowers in orange, gold, or white. And, like the small marigolds, you can pick entire branching stems rather than individual flowers.

Warm-season annuals can't stand cold nights. Wait to sow seed outdoors or plant them in the cutting garden until night temperatures stay reliably above 50°F, or they may stunt. It's worth waiting to set them out because these warm-season annuals, which generally originated in tropical and subtropical climates, bloom through the heat of summer and often well into autumn.

WARM-SEASON ANNUALS FOR CUTTING

- **African marigold** *(Tagetes erecta)*
  These large-flowered kinds of marigold have the longest stems; select yellow, gold, primrose, or cream.

- **Ageratum** *(Ageratum houstonianum)*
  Old-fashioned blue 'Cut Wonder' grows more than a foot tall and makes the best cut flower.

- **Bachelor's button** *(Centaurea cyanus)*
  Classic blue on long, thin stems for purists; mixture of pink, white, lavender, maroon, and blue is equally delightful.

- **Balsam** *(Impatiens balsamina)*
  Related to impatiens but on stems up to a foot or more with single or double flowers in pink, purple, salmon, pink, white, and combinations.

- **Bishop's weed** *(Ammi majus)*
  Much like Queen Anne's lace with umbels of feathery white flowers but blooms earlier; easy from seed or transplants.

- **Blue lace flower** *(Trachymene caerulea)*
  Long stems and charming flowers, like powder blue Queen Anne's lace.

- **China aster** *(Callistephus chinensis)*
  Select tallest forms for the best cutting; single or double flowers in pink, purple, and white.

- **Cleome** or **spider flower** *(Cleome hasslerana)*
  Long stems studded with pink or white flowers with spidery stamens.

- **Coleus** *(Coleus blumei)*
  Though the flowers are insignificant, the plain or patterned leaves in chartreuse, red, bronze, and green are good fillers in bouquets.

- **Cosmos** *(Cosmos bipinnatus)*
  One of the all-time easiest cut flowers; scatter seed and harvest hundreds of white, pink, or magenta beauties on long, wiry stems.

- **Gloriosa daisy** or **annual black-eyed Susan** *(Rudbeckia hirta)*
  Single or semidouble daisies with classic gold petals or rustic shades of russet brown or burnt orange.

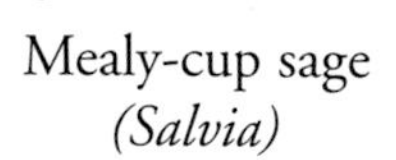

Mealy-cup sage
(Salvia)

- **Mealy-cup sage** *(Salvia farinacea)*
  Cut an entire branch for good effect; classic dusty blue is a favorite but also white and bicolor hybrids.

- **Mexican sunflower** *(Tithonia rotundifolia)*
  Tall as regular sunflowers with long-stemmed orange-petaled single blooms.

Cosmos tolerates poor soil, drought, and neglect but still offers myriad flowers for cutting, mixed here with double hollyhocks.

- **Salvia** *(Salvia splendens)*
  Grow the tallest kinds for best cutting; if you can't stand the scarlet, there are softer shades of salmon, eggplant purple, and white.

- **Sunflower** *(Helianthus annuus)*
  A wide variety of singles and doubles in yellow, gold, deep red, and orange tones; select taller sorts for the longest stems.

- **Tall verbena** *(Verbena patagonica,* syn. *V. bonariensis)*
  Clusters of tiny lavender-purple flowers atop straight, leafless stems add airy dimension to arrangements.

- **Zinnia** *(Zinnia elegans)*
  Select tallest varieties for longest stems; plant a mixture for many colors or single color hybrids in your favorite shades of red, gold, orange, pink, or white.

ANNUALS, BIENNIALS, AND TENDER PERENNIALS FOR SHADE

Caladium
(Caladium)

- **Caladium** *(Caladium × hortolanum)*
  The flowers are inconspicuous, but the large, veined leaves in tropical shades of red, green, and white are dramatic.

- **Candytuft** *(Iberis umbellata)*
  Like the popular perennial but in pretty colors of pink, mauve, lavender, and white.

- **Coleus** *(Coleus blumei)*
  The varied leaves in many colors and patterns add pizzazz to bouquets.

An early summer bouquet freshly cut from the garden includes alliums, goatsbeard, honeysuckle, meadow rue, spuria iris, salvia, and yellow foxgloves.

Foxglove
(Digitalis)

- **Foxglove** *(Digitalis purpurea)*
  The 'Foxy' strain blooms the first year from seed with classic white, lavender, or pink bells on long stems.

- **Heliotrope** *(Heliotropium arborescens)*
  Large, scented clusters of small flowers in purple, lavender, or white.

Honesty
(Lunaria)

- **Honesty** *(Lunaria annua)*
  Enjoy the simple, four-petaled pink or white flowers or wait for the translucent silver seedpods. A biennial, flowers the second year.

- **Love-in-a-mist** *(Nigella damascena)*
  Pretty blue, white, or mulberry pink flowers enclosed in a mist of finely cut foliage; stems are relatively short.

- **Pansy** *(Viola wittrockiana)*
  Charming faces in many colors for small bouquets; flower production improves with constant picking.

- **Queen Anne's lace** *(Daucus carota)*
  Long-stemmed lacy white domes that continue well into autumn add an airiness when used in arrangements.

- **Wax begonia** *(Begonia semperflorens)*
  Pick sprays of red, pink, or white flowers with green or bronze leaves attached for maximum effect.

- **Wishbone flower** *(Torenia fournieri)*
  Short but sweet flowers somewhat like pansies in blue or shades of pink, white, and cream.

- **Woodland tobacco** *(Nicotiana sylvestris)*
  Tall stems support large candelabra flower heads of fragrant tubular flowers.

A high-altitude cutting garden includes sweet Williams, Iceland poppies, pansies, and pinks.

ANNUALS FOR HIGH-ALTITUDE OR COOL REGIONS

- **Dusty miller** *(Senecio cineraria)*
  Start with transplants and use liberally in arrangements for silver foliage contrast.

Flowering tobacco *(Nicotiana)*

- **Flowering tobacco** *(Nicotiana alata)*
  Pick the whole head of starry flowers in pink, red, salmon, white, lavender, or chartreuse; start with transplants.

- **Gloriosa daisy** or **annual black-eyed Susan** *(Rudbeckia hirta)*
  Gold or brownish daisy flowers, bigger than the wildflower; start with transplants.

- **Honesty** *(Lunaria annua)*
  Most valued for the silver dollar seed heads; leave some to self-sow.

- **Iceland poppy** *(Papaver nudicaule)*
  Survives transplanting but easiest grown from fall-scattered seed; tolerates frost well.

- **Love-in-a-mist** *(Nigella damascena)*
  Though not too tall (up to 1 foot), the blue, pink, or white flowers are useful for small bouquets; leave some to self-sow.

- **Nemesia** *(Nemesia strumosa)*
  Up to a foot tall with small cups of white, pale blue, yellow, bronze, pink, red, or lavender; cut entire branch for best effect.

Painted tongue (Salpiglossis sinuata) *revels in cool temperatures and brilliant sunshine, making it an ideal plant for high-altitude cutting gardens.*

- **Painted tongue** *(Salpiglossis sinuata)*
  Imagine petunias with vibrant golden veining on velvety trumpets of purple, scarlet, rose, blue, and mahogany; tallest strains are best for cutting.

- **Pansy** *(Viola wittrockiana)*
  Most gardeners set out transplants in autumn and hope snow cover insulates them until spring; cover with pine boughs if snowfall is inadequate.

- **Pincushion flower** *(Scabiosa atropurpurea)*
  Similar to perennial pincushion flowers but in a wider range of colors including pink, white, salmon, red, powder blue, and maroon-black on long, wiry stems.

Snapdragons in many shades share a sunny space with corn and other vegetables.

- **Pinks** *(Dianthus chinensis)*
  Annual forms of garden pinks come in pink, red, white, and bicolors; spicy scent for small bouquets.

- **Poor man's orchid** *(Schizanthus wisetonensis)*
  Gorgeous little butterfly-like flowers in jewel tones of pink, crimson, violet, purple, or white, all veined in gold; select tallest strains and use entire stems; start with transplants.

Poor man's orchid
(Schizanthus)

- **Pot marigold** *(Calendula officinalis)*
  Double or single daisies in vibrant yellow or orange; avoid dwarf strains if you want long stems.

- **Rocky Mountain garland** *(Clarkia elegans)*
  Long straight stems clad with spidery single flowers or double, camellia-like blossoms in salmon, hot pink, white, mauve, or lavender.

- **Satin flower** *(Godetia amoena)*
  Elegant red, pink, or white flowers like poppies on stems up to a foot tall.

- **Shirley poppy** *(Papaver rhoeas)*
  Sow seed in fall for spring crop.

- **Snapdragon** *(Antirrhinum majus)*
  Almost unlimited color range ideal for cutting; select mixtures or single colors; start with transplants.

- **Stock** *(Matthiola incana)*
  Select tallest strains for longest cuts; double or single blossoms in pink, white, lavender, or cream are deliciously fragrant.

- **Sweet pea** *(Lathyrus odoratus)*
  Will continue blooming if well watered, fertilized, and picked.

Clove-scented stock (Matthiola incana) *invites butterflies and flower arrangers.*

Climbing roses take advantage of a simple fence of lattice and an old wagon wheel surrounding a cutting garden with yarrow, ornamental grasses, foxgloves, and penstemon.

Roses

When flower arrangers think of their favorite flowers, the rose nearly always comes first to mind. Hybrid tea roses are among the most labor-intensive flowers, so don't count your bouquets before they're picked. Experiment with classic varieties first, such as crimson 'Mr. Lincoln', yellow and peach 'Peace', or wonderfully fragrant red and white 'Double Delight'. Don't expect to pick a dozen long-stemmed beauties at any given moment from one bush, but fertilizer, water, and insect and disease control (plus a little prayer) will probably make your experiments worthwhile. Remember, just one rose in a simple bud vase can be as lovely as a whole bouquet.

While hybrid tea roses command the most attention, the old-fashioned shrub and floribunda roses can be equally rewarding. These are picked in clusters, such as those early summer-flowering varieties like orange and yellow 'Austrian Copper', yellow 'Persian Yellow' and 'Harrison's Yellow', or white *Rosa alba*. Rugosa roses, such 'Therese Bugnet', are delightfully fragrant and repeat throughout the summer.

The problem with shrub roses in the cutting garden is space. Most of us don't have room for many shrubs that grow 6, 8, or 10 feet wide and as high. Some of the smaller floribunda or landscape roses can be more easily fit into a cutting garden. These include pale pink 'The Fairy', coral pink 'Ferdy', or the Meidiland series in pink, red, or white. Climbers such as pale pink 'New Dawn' or 'Maiden's Blush' or red 'Blaze' can scramble up an arbor or archway trellis in a pretty way while saving space.

Summer Shrubs

- **Beauty bush** *(Kolkwitzia amabilis)*
  Lovely pale coral-pink flowers nearly obscure the small leaves.

- **Butterfly bush** *(Buddleia alternifolia, B. davidii)*
  Spires of flowers resemble lilacs and come in purple, pink, white, and lavender-blue.

Butterfly bush *(Buddleia)*

- **Carolina allspice** *(Calycanthus floridus)*
  Odd burgundy-brown flowers feature spicy "aftershave" fragrance.

- **Caryopteris** *(Caryopteris × clandonensis, C. incana)*
  Tiers of fluffy blue flowers produced prolifically throughout late summer and autumn.

- **Ceanothus** (*Ceanothus* spp.)
  Lovely trusses of pale blue flowers look a bit like lilacs; often seen on the West Coast.

- **Clethra** (*Clethra* spp.)
  Graceful pink or white spires of sweetly scented small flowers.

Sweet pepper bush *(Clethra)*

*Butterfly bush (*Buddleia *'Nanho White') produces elegant spires in summer, complemented by airy purple* Verbena patagonica *and* Nicotiana sylvestris.

- **Elder** *(Sambucus caerulea, S. canadensis)*
  The heads of white flowers look like loose clusters of hydrangea; subsequent berries are also ornamental.

- **Fernbush** *(Chamaebatiaria millefolium)*
  For dry areas. Spikes of cream flowers are complemented by olive green ferny leaves.

- **Mock orange** (*Philadelphus* spp.)
  Enchanting citruslike fragrance of single or double white flowers transforms any bouquet.

- **Oleander** (*Olearia* spp.)
  Pink, red, white, or peach-pink flowers add tropical touch to arrangements; flowers are freely produced over a long period; a staple in California.

- **Potentilla** (*Potentilla* spp.)
  Five-petaled yellow, pink, white, or orange blossoms on arching stems blooming over an extended period.

- **Sorbus** (*Sorbus* spp.)
  Spires of small cream flowers look like lilacs but without the scent; tolerates shade.

- **Spirea** (*Spiraea* spp.)
  Many species and forms in white, pink, and dusty rose [illegible]
  Small flowers are produced in flat, round heads.

Spirea
(Spiraea)

- **Viburnum** (*Viburnum* spp.)
  Many species in white or pale pink, often with carnation-like fragrance; many are shade-tolerant.

Viburnum
(Viburnum)

- **Weigela** (*Weigela* spp.)
  Red, white, or pink flowers are freely produced over a long period.

PEONIES

Early summer is peony season. It's wonderful to bury one's nose in their plush petals. Doubles are usually the most fragrant, such as the classic pink 'Sarah Bernhardt' or the red-flecked white 'Festiva Maxima'. These heavy flowers test the strength of their stems. A firm wire peony hoop or substantial twine and bamboo cage helps support them. Single peonies like pink 'Seashell' or 'Crinkled White' are equally lovely, as are the anemone-flowering types. These flowers have broad outer petals and a fluffy center. 'Bowl of Beauty' is pink with a white center, 'Nippon Beauty' is maroon red, and 'Primevere' features white outer petals surrounding a lemon yellow center.

Tree peonies are small, woody shrubs that, unlike their garden peony cousins, don't die down to the roots each winter. Tree peonies have been bred in Asia for many centuries; their huge, sumptuous blossoms are breathtaking. Though scentless, the flowers make beautiful bouquets and are dazzling floated in a pretty bowl.

For many gardeners, Memorial Day isn't complete without a bouquet of peonies, such as striking 'Bowl of Beauty'.

SUMMER PERENNIALS FOR CUTTING

The daisy family heads the list of perennials that provide a nonstop supply of fresh flowers. In addition to the familiar varieties of Shasta daisy, flower arrangers can count on many members of the daisy family, such as tickseed (*Coreopsis* spp.), black-eyed Susan (*Rudbeckia* spp.), painted daisy (*Pyrethrum* spp.), snow daisy *(Tanacetum niveum),* purple coneflower *(Echinacea purpurea),* feverfew *(Tanacetum parthenium),* anthemis, Indian blanket *(Gaillardia aristata),* Mexican hat *(Ratibida columnifera),* cupid's dart *(Catananche caerulea),* false sunflower (*Heliopsis* spp.), and Helen's flower *(Helenium autumnale).*

Showy, upright perennials help to create tall, dramatic bouquets — the type that look wonderful on a mantle or showcased on a pedestal. Delphiniums in shades of blue, purple, and white are traditional favorites. They should be staked from early in the season to ensure wind or rain doesn't break them before they're ready to cut. A similar look may be achieved by cutting monkshood (*Aconitum* spp.), usually noted for their somber, deep indigo or purple blossoms.

Lupines *(Lupinus)* are a bit jollier, coming in a veritable rainbow of colors, including white, yellow, pink, blue, and purple. Hybridizers have also bred two-tone combinations, such as pink and white or blue and yellow. The tiered flowers of bee balm *(Monarda didyma)* also provide important vertical accents in an arrangement. Though most gardeners are familiar with the common red sorts, there's a range of more subtle bee balm shades, from pink and white to lavender and mahogany red.

Red-hot poker *(Kniphofia uvaria)* bears spikes of vivid orange tubular flowers. For those who might find these too bold, the hybrid 'Primrose Beauty' bears moonlight yellow flowers. Some gardeners also cut the spectacular spikes of yuccas for bouquets. The white or cream white blossoms are spectacular. Western gardeners enjoy the tubular bells of *Penstemon,* especially scarlet bugler *(P. barbatus),* pink or white shell-leaf penstemon *(P. palmeri),* and grape blue Rocky Mountain penstemon *(P. strictus).*

Fluffy-flowered perennials provide a useful counterpoint to vertical flowers or to lilies and roses. Baby's breath *(Gypsophila paniculata)* is the quintessential flower used for softening a bouquet and accenting the larger flowers. Goatsbeard *(Aruncus dioicus)* offers creamy white plumes that may be used in a similar manner. The tiny flowers of meadow rue *(Thalictrum aquilegifolium)* are

clustered together in airy, irregular clusters of lavender or white. The flower heads of plume poppy *(Macleaya cordata)* are equally delicate in appearance. Its small flowers are an unusual shade of salmon brown (connoisseurs take note) and mature into attractive seed heads later on in the season.

Russian sage *(Perovskia atriplicifolia),* blooming in midsummer and into autumn, provides misty blue flowers on upright stems that provide a gauzy backdrop for other blossoms. Some species of sage, such as *Salvia nemorosa* and *S. verticillata,* make good cut flowers, noted for their soft spikes of purple, blue, or pink flowers. Cultivars of veronica *(Veronica spicata)* such as white 'Icicle' or 'Crater Lake Blue' also contribute a fine-textured column of tiny flowers. Some of the taller catmints *(Nepeta)* such as *N. sibirica,* 'Six Hills Giant' or 'Walker's Low', also have branches long enough for cutting with a haze of misty blue flowers. Another good filler perennial is *Filipendula,* including meadowsweet *(F. ulmaria),* with clusters of ivory white flowers, or queen-of-the-meadow (*F. venusta* 'Rubra'), which makes puffs of tiny pink flowers with the texture of cotton candy. For a delicate jolt of color, the fine sprays of coralbells *(Heuchera)* can be inserted easily into an almost-finished bouquet. Most of us think of the bright red variety, but some cultivars offer pink, peach, or white bells.

No cutting garden is complete without yarrow. The tall golden flowers of *Achillea coronaria* make vibrant companions for purple delphiniums or monkshood. The pale flowers of *A. tagetya* 'Moonshine' or 'Anthea' serve the same purpose in a pastel bouquet, with their plates of tightly clustered flowers tucked in against spiky snapdragons or gladiolus. Even more color options are provided by hybrids of *A. millefolium.* This easily grown perennial (all yarrows are easy as pie and often too willing to thrive) now comes in a number of selected cultivars besides the common white or pale pink species. 'Cerise Queen' is deep pink, 'Lavender Lady' is aptly named, and 'Paprika' is orange-red. At least a dozen other cultivars allow an arranger to select exactly the right shade. The 'Summer Pastel' mixture offers a lovely variety of flowers in salmon pink, buff, pale yellow, sandstone pink, and ivory. Last but not least, *A. ptarmica* is an old-fashioned perennial with pretty double white blossoms similar to the other yarrows but in looser clusters.

Lady's mantle *(Alchemilla vulgaris)* and lady's-bedstraw *(Galium vernum)* are valued for their unique coloration. Lady's mantle produces a foam of tiny char-

Beautiful shell-leaf penstemon (Penstemon palmeri) *thrives in a dry, sunny site with annual pinks* (Dianthus barbatus).

treuse flowers and seems to bring out the best in its companions, be they pink peonies, blue irises, or red roses. Lady's-bedstraw has similar flowers that start out bright yellow and fade to chartreuse. It can be used much like lady's-mantle and has longer, more rigid stems (although the whole plant often flops in the garden, calling for a support network of twigs or wire).

Soft, plush flowers produced on single stems are invaluable in bouquets. Pincushion flower *(Scabiosa caucasica),* in blue, lavender, white, or pink, features large outside petals with a center that resembles, well, a pincushion. The long, wiry stems make them ideal for cutting and arranging. Burgundy pincushion flower *(Knautia macedonica)* looks almost the same except for its dramatic color. By contrast, giant pincushion flower (*Cephelaria alpina* and *C. gigantea*) produces similar flowers in a pleasing shade of butter yellow on exceptionally long stems. Perennial bachelor's buttons contribute soft, shaggy flowers. Those of *Centaurea dealbata* are pink, *C. montana*'s are cobalt blue or white, and those of *C. macrocephala* are golden yellow.

The prickly texture of sea holly (*Eryngium* spp.) and globe thistle *(Echinops ritro)* contrast effectively with many other flowers. The steely blue color of both sea holly and globe thistle is also desirable in a pastel grouping with pink or yellow. Arrangers who love blue flowers (one can never have too many) can turn to the bellflowers. Peach-leaf bellflower *(Campanula persicifolia)* is one of the best. Its Spode blue bells are always delightful in early summer; there's also a white variety. For smaller arrangements, harebell *(C. rotundifolia)* is almost like a miniature version with small blue bells. Milky bellflower *(C. lactiflora)* has clusters of bells in soft shades of lavender-blue, mauve, and white. *C. punctata* is creamy pink with darker spots inside, while *C. latifolia* offers splendid tall spikes of long, flared bells in purple or white.

The list of summer-flowering perennials that make good cut flowers is extensive, but I do have a few more personal favorites. Great billowing heads of garden phlox *(Phlox paniculata),* usually with the soft scent like baby powder, are almost bouquets by themselves. I especially like pure white 'David' and 'Mt. Fuji', but who can resist the soft pink blossoms with a darker center of 'Brilliant Eye' or the rosy purple flowers of 'Amethyst'? Everyone has a favorite phlox — usually the one that gets the least mildew. In the cutting garden, the curse of mildew is not quite as problematic as in a border. We can cut the stems and strip away the offending leaves.

Bouquets reach new heights of glory in summer when dahlias, phlox, and cleome hit their stride.

Another favorite perennial is sweet William *(Dianthus barbatus),* though it's considered a biennial or short-lived perennial. I love the spicy, clovelike scent of the flower heads. They're perfect for stuffing together in an old tea pot or beer stein. The colors are mainly shades of pink and red, including bicolors, with a smattering of white thrown in. I don't grow any carnations — I leave that to the professionals — but many members of the *Dianthus* genus make great cut flowers. Most of the garden perennials aren't as showy as their highly bred carnation cousins, nor are their stems as long, but such species as cottage pinks *(D. plumarius)* and maiden pinks *(D. deltoides)* make lovely smaller bouquets.

Biennials for Cutting

Canterbury bell
(Campanula)

Canterbury bell *(Campanula medium)*
Plump pink, white, or blue bells on tall stems; stake to prevent rain or wind damage.

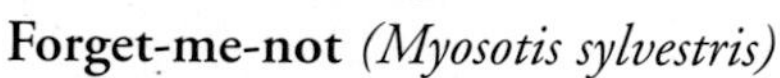

Forget-me-not *(Myosotis sylvestris)*
Although it will bloom the first year from seed if planted early, it is usually grown as a biennial; self-sows.

Foxglove *(Digitalis purpurea)*
Spires of spotted, tubular flowers in white, pink, mauve, and apricot; leave some to self-sow.

Brown-eyed Susan *(Rudbeckia triloba)*
Tall, late-season clusters of brilliant gold, black-eyed flowers; cut entire branches.

Sweet rocket *(Hesperis matronalis)*
Fragrant single flowers of bright pink or white are held in clusters on branching stems.

Sweet William *(Dianthus barbatus)*
Thick stems support heads of spicy flowers in white, pink, red, or maroon, sometimes with contrasting zigzag edges.

Though short-lived, sweet William is worth the effort to replant every other year for its clusters of spicy sweet blossoms.

Perennials for Partial Shade

When the cutting garden is positioned in partial shade, there are still many perennials that produce during the summer. Goatsbeard *(Aruncus dioicus),* monkshood (*Aconitum* spp.), and meadowsweet (*Filipendula* spp.) grow well in shadier conditions. Other good candidates include *Astilbe* spp., masterwort (*Astrantia* spp.), columbine (*Aquilegia* spp.), cardinal flower *(Lobelia cardinalis),* and hosta. The latter provide great leaves and pretty flowers in lavender or white. Some are softly scented, but *Hosta plantaginea* is noted for large white flowers with an intoxicating smell (reminding me of a combination of orange blossoms and jasmine). The double form 'Aphrodite' is equally fragrant and a bit showier in bouquets.

D. × *allwoodii* is a group of hybrids created by crossing carnations with cottage pinks. Splendid as garden perennials and as cut flowers, they include salmon pink 'Helen', pale pink 'Daphne', red 'Ian', and reddish orange 'Robin'.

SUMMER BULBS

Summer-flowering bulbs come in many shapes, sizes, and scents. Most home flower arrangers would never dream of picking an onion for a bouquet—but they should. The ornamental onions make wonderful, long-lasting cut flowers. These alliums include lavender-purple *Allium giganteum* (with very long stems for very grand arrangements), pale violet *A. cristophii* (with round heads almost the size of a cantaloupe), maroon drumstick allium (with oval heads the size of a kiwi fruit on long, stiff stems), *A. caeruleum* (its small round flower heads compensate with flowers of intense true blue), and *A. aflatunense* (purple, lavender, or white flowers on round heads the size of baseballs). Though these are all members of the onion family, they have little or no smell unless bruised. Alliums may also be left to dry and used in everlasting arrangements. Some gardeners tint the dried rounded heads with spray paint.

On the West Coast, lily-of-the-Nile *(Agapanthus)* and Peruvian lily *(Alstroemeria)* have found homes in many landscapes. They may have become almost as familiar as petunias or marigolds in the rest of the country, but they have distinctive flowers that last exceedingly well when cut. Most gardeners are familiar with the common blue agapanthus (a beautiful Wedgwood blue), but there are also white forms and a deep violet blue called 'Storm Cloud'. Alstroemeria also grow well across most of the southern part of the nation—as far north as Zone 6—and the lovely flowers are among the longest lasting of all cut flowers, fluttering above long, sturdy stems to boot. The individual blossoms appear to have been marked with the precision of a fine artist's brush in rows of alternating dashes. The colors are lovely—from white and pastel peach, pink, and yellow to bold orange, gold, bronze, and many combinations in between.

Gladiolus, once a mainstay of almost every American garden, has lately fallen from favor. In a perennial border, the spectacular hybrid good looks of gladiolus may fit in about as well as Las Vegas showgirls at a folk dance, but they make ideal cut flowers. There's much to recommend them for the cutting garden, for they are easy to grow, are inexpensive, and come in a huge variety of colors. Some are pastel—pink, lavender, pale yellow, white, salmon pink—while others are vibrant fiery tones of red, orange, and gold. Still others are chartreuse green or purple, and many varieties sport showy two-tone color combinations. They last for a long time and provide important vertical accents in a large arrangement. Perhaps they've been badly displayed in the past, with a dozen or more stalks splayed out like the plumage of a peacock by unimaginative wedding florists, but they can be arranged in a much more casual way, especially combined with softening clods of phlox, grasses, butterfly bush, and yarrow. I find the individual flowers so pretty that I sometimes cut them off the stems and float them in a large seashell or crystal bowl.

Some gardeners have a special affection for *Gladiolus byzantinus,* an old-fashioned favorite with carmine pink flowers. It has smaller flowers on shorter stems but is still good for cutting. Where hardy—often to Zone 5—it often makes itself at home in the poorest of clay soils and multiplies and persists with little care. The nanus gladiolus are similar to *G. byzantinus* and may prove hardy where gladiolus seldom are. Like *G. byzantinus,* the stems are usually only 15 to 18 inches long with pretty flowers in shades of white, pink, and red, often with striking contrasting markings on the petals.

An interesting species of gladiolus is a bit less bold than the hybrids. Abyssinian gladiolus (*Gladiolus callicanthus*, formerly called *Acidanthera bicolor*) features

graceful, open, white flowers with striking maroon centers. Rather than being clustered tightly on a thick stalk like the hybrids, the flowers are spaced farther apart and are held on slender, curved stems. An added bonus is the soft, sweet scent. As easy to grow as the hybrids, Abyssinnian gladiolus is ideal for the cutting garden. So are montbretia and crocosmia. With spearlike leaves like gladiolus, these bulbs glow in shades of scarlet, orange, gold, and yellow. Montbretia (properly *Crocosmia* × *crocosmiflora*) have open, starry small flowers held in sprays, while crocosmia have arching wands thickly studded with small, tubular flowers. Fiery red *Crocosmia masonorum* 'Lucifer' is one of the most popular sorts.

Dahlias, like gladiolus, have been subject to the whims of fashion, falling and rising with the regularity of women's hemlines. They're currently back in vogue, perhaps because flower arrangers have discovered how varied the dahlia family is. They range from the giant behemoths with flowers the size of a dinner plate to the smaller pompons and singles. And like gladiolus, dahlias come in an astonishing range of shades and color combinations. The smaller-flowered dahlias such as the single red 'Bishop of Llandaff' or orange 'Ellen Houston' offer a smaller, less overpowering flower that combines easily with other cut flowers. The giants are so imposing that they stand out all by themselves. These are usually classified as giant dinner plate, giant decorative, and cactus-flowering types. Specialists break these divisions down even further, but it all gets a bit confusing, so I'm sticking with the most general types. Dahlia fanatics who like their flowers as large as possible "disbud" their plants. They remove all but one bud on each stem to force the dahlia to put all of its energy into a single enormous blossom. The results of their efforts are often exhibited at county and state fairs, but it's generally too much work for the average home gardener.

Classics in the dinner plate department include yellow 'Kelvin Floodlight', 'Lavender Perfection', and orange 'Babylon Bronze'. Decorative types (smaller but no less spectacular than the dinner plate types) include purple 'Thomas A. Edison', rose with white tips 'Jean Marie', and yellow-edged red 'Flowerfield'. Among the cactus-flowered group, consistent winners include yellow-tipped red 'Firebird', yellow 'Promise', and pink 'Park Princess'. The latter is one of the shorter types, growing to a mere 2 feet in height, whereas many larger-flowered dahlias may grow to 4 or 5 feet or more, depending on conditions. A relatively new class is the powder puff type, once known as anemone type. A collar of large outer petals encircles a "puff" of many tightly clustered smaller petals.

Smaller types of gladiolus, often known as nanus or baby gladiolus, fit more gracefully into arrangements than their taller cousins.

Though large dahlias are most often grown for the show bench, they're obvious candidates for the cutting garden. Strong stakes are highly recommended. Experts often "plant" the stake at the same time as the tubers, in deep holes supplemented liberally with compost. As the plants grow, they are covered up several times as the new shoots hit several inches high. This ensures a strong underground structure, although it is never enough to keep them from needing additional support. The stake should be a strong pole sunk at least a foot deep. The plant is tethered to it as it grows; some veterans prefer strips of old nylon stockings because the fabric is both soft and strong. Single, pompon, and some of the cactus group usually don't require staking.

To get the most out of your dahlias as cut flowers, sear the end of each stem with a flame, then plunge them all the way up to the neck of the flower in cool to tepid water, leaving them immersed for at least 3 hours. Some gardeners prefer to wait a full day. This ensures that the hollow stems don't collapse.

Peruvian daffodil *(Hymenocallis)* does indeed resemble a spring daffodil, albeit a rather exotic one. Several species and hybrids are available; the common white *H. aestivus* is pure white with graceful, drooping petals surrounding the flower cup. Its scent is enchanting. Pale yellow 'Sulfur Queen' is slightly smaller and the petals aren't as long. Both have thick, hollow stalks like an amaryllis with three or more blossoms clustered at the top. Peruvian daffodil is hardy only in mild winter areas where the temperature rarely falls below freezing. Elsewhere, dig and store the bulbs over winter like gladiolus.

Species of *Liatris,* sometimes called blazing star or Kansas gayfeather, make rewarding, long-lasting cut flowers. The plants grow from corms, and the ramrod-straight stems are clad in fluffy white or purple flowers. Whereas almost all other flowers arranged on upright stems, such as delphinium or monkshood, open from the bottom upward, liatris flower in reverse, starting at the top. Another great vertical accent is the pineapple lily *(Eucomis punctata).* Its long stems are studded with small, star-shaped flowers in cream, pale green, or plum pink. A tuft of green foliage like that of a pineapple rests at the top, giving the flower its common name. Like liatris, pineapple lilies last longer than most flowers in arrangements. While liatris is hardy across most of the country, pineapple lilies must be dug and stored north of Zone 7.

Tuberoses *(Polyanthes tuberosa)* used to be great favorites, but they aren't grown much these days. That's too bad. From a rosette of yuccalike foliage, tuberoses produce stiff stalks studded with single white flowers, usually blooming from late summer into fall. Their sweet scent is magical, though sometimes a bit overwhelming for those with sensitive noses (which may help to explain their fall from grace). A double form of tuberose called 'The Pearl' has creamy flowers with a soft salmon pink blush. Tuberoses are as easy to grow as gladiolus, but they have the annoying habit of splitting into small, non-blooming–size bulblets at the end of the season. Since the bulbs are inexpensive, it's worth it to purchase new ones each spring.

Lilies

The biggest stars of the summer-flowering bulbs are the lilies. Among the first are the martagons *(Lilium martagon),* with tiny Turk's-cap flowers in plum or white, and the Chinese coral lily *(L. pumilum),* which is similar but brilliant, waxy orange. *Lilium hansonii* is also similar but features vibrant golden yellow flowers. The white Madonna lily *(L. candidum)* also blooms early.

The Asiatic hybrids come next, through early summer into July. They are grouped by their upfacing, outfacing, or downfacing flowers. The colors are nearly as unlimited as the rainbow, except for blue. The hues range from white, pastel peach, pink, and cream to intense orange, yellow, and red. Bicolors (with two or more colors on each petal) are very showy, and some lilies feature freckles and spots. Some gardeners especially favor the lilies marked with "brushmarks," usually brown or reddish marks that appear to have been applied by

Selected Asiatic Lilies for Cutting

Apollo: upfacing white with black spots
Ariadne: downfacing dusty rose
Brushstroke: upfacing white with plum "brushmarks"
Cherry Smash: upfacing cherry red
Chianti: upfacing pink
Citronella: downfacing yellow with brown spots
Doeskin: outfacing buff
Fireworks: outfacing orange-red
Flirt: upfacing yellow with plum "brushmarks"
Hornpipe: upfacing melon orange
Joanna: upfacing golden yellow
Last Dance: downfacing yellow
Plum Crazy: upfacing plum pink with ivory tips
Red Velvet: outfacing maroon red
Tiger Babies: outfacing peach with brown spots
Tinkerbell: downfacing pink
Yellow Blaze: upfacing yellow

brush on the inner part of the petals. While most Asiatic lilies have no fragrance, hybridizers have recently crossed them with the Easter lily. The result is a new breed of lightly scented Asiatic hybrids. 'Royal Highness' is pale peach, 'My Fair Lady' is pink, 'Royal Perfume' is cantaloupe orange, 'Royal Dream' is ivory yellow, and 'Kiss Me Kate' is coral rose.

Fragrance is unmistakable in the trumpet lilies (sometimes called Aurelians) that follow the Asiatics in bloom sequence. Most are quite tall (though breeders have begun to produce shorter varieties) and are noted for large, graceful trumpets with intoxicating fragrance. White, yellow, pink, gold, and orange are the main colors, often with dramatic maroon petals on the outside of the trumpet. 'Summer Palace' is pink, 'White Henryi' is white with orange centers, 'Golden Sceptre' is golden yellow with bronze reverse, 'Lady Anne' is apricot with ivory tips, 'Copper King' is melon orange, 'Midnight' is mauve-purple, and 'Black Dragon' is white with maroon-brown reverse.

Selected Oriental Lilies for Cutting

Allura: light pink with darker spots
Bessie: rose red with darker spots
Coral Bee: coral pink
Harbor Star: white with orange and pink stripe
Imperial Gold: white with gold bands and brown spots
Journey's End: crimson pink
Lemon Meringue: white with gold bands
Marco Polo: pale pink
Oregon Mist: white with maroon spots
Pink Ribbons: rose with deeper bands, spots
Red Jamboree: red with white edge
Salmon Jewels: yellow blending to pale salmon pink
Sans Souci: white with rose spots
Sweet Frost: white with red spots
Tickled Pink: pale pink

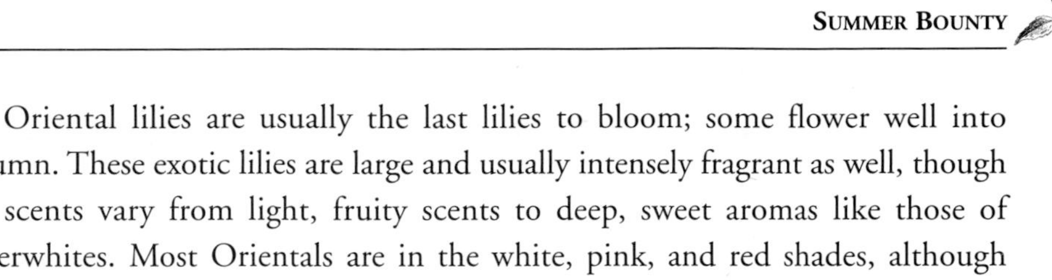

Oriental lilies are usually the last lilies to bloom; some flower well into autumn. These exotic lilies are large and usually intensely fragrant as well, though the scents vary from light, fruity scents to deep, sweet aromas like those of paperwhites. Most Orientals are in the white, pink, and red shades, although some have pretty yellow bands on the petals. Most also feature striking patterns of spots. Many gardeners are familiar with the Oriental "rubrum" lilies. Other gardeners know the classic 'Stargazer', which is a florist's best friend. They are easily grown at home, as are dozens of hybrids with great scent and beauty. Classic Oriental hybrids include white 'Casablanca', crimson-pink 'Journey's End', and dark red 'Black Beauty'.

Almost all lilies have brown or cinnamon-red pollen that, when shed, stains tablecloths and clothing. Florists customarily snip off the anthers that carry the pollen. Home gardeners should do the same (although most gardeners agree it looks peculiar) or display a bouquet of lilies on a wooden, glass, or marble surface that can be easily wiped clean.

Madonna lily
(Lilium)

CHAPTER 5
AUTUMN GLORIES

For some gardeners, autumn marks the beginning of the end, but the cutting garden continues to heat up. The annuals just keep blooming, perhaps even more prolifically than before. It may be that a touch of cool in the evening signals them to hurry up and set seed. The annuals are joined by a parade of late-blooming perennials. Many are as flamboyant as any flower that spring or summer can offer. In addition, those plants that have already bloomed now display fascinating fruit and berries as well as pods and seed heads. Perennials, shrubs, and trees begin to display their brilliant fall foliage.

ANNUALS FOR FALL BOUQUETS

The cutting garden in autumn is stuffed with enough flowers to supply the whole neighborhood with bouquets. Sunflowers in all shades from pale yellow to rusty maroon bloom like crazy. Mexican sunflower *(Tithonia rotundifolia)* often towers above the rest, blooming in bright, nearly fluorescent orange. The dahlias

A multipurpose cutting garden accommodates tall African marigolds, sunflowers, and cosmos as well as zucchini and pumpkins.

(also originally from Mexico) keep up their flowering as long as hot afternoons prevail. And while we're on the subject of Mexican flowers, where would a cutting garden be without two other natives — marigolds and zinnias?

Some people don't care for the smell of marigolds, but I've always liked it. A whiff is like a bracing splash of after-shave lotion. Some varieties aren't quite as pungent, but those who dislike the smell should probably exclude marigolds from their cutting beds. Shorter varieties, often called French or signet marigolds, are almost too short-stemmed for cutting, though late in the season an entire branch may be cut. I prefer 'Lemon Gem' or 'Tangerine Gem' for this purpose. The taller sorts — often seen in city park bedding schemes — are much more suitable for cutting. These are usually called African marigolds (with the French and African designations, it's no wonder that most people don't know marigolds are native to Mexico). The tall varieties come in orange, lemon yellow, and very pale yellow (the result of a breeder's fruitless quest for a white marigold).

Other annuals that continue well into autumn with an abundance of blossoms are zinnias *(Zinnia elegans),* mealy-cup sage *(Salvia farinacea),* spider flower *(Cleome hasslerana),* annual black-eyed Susan *(Rudbeckia hirta),* Queen Anne's lace *(Daucus carota),* annual pincushion flower *(Scabiosa atropurpurea),* verbenas, and flowering tobacco *(Nicotiana alata).* The shorter hybrid types of flowering tobacco such as the 'Domino' and 'Starship' series bloom in white, chartreuse, pink, salmon, red, and dull purple. For best effect, they can be picked at the base for a showy cluster. The tall woodland tobacco *(N. sylvestris)* produces candelabra of tubular white flowers on tall stems. They're dramatic in large arrangements.

Seedpods

Some annuals that have finished blooming have unique seedpods. Love-in-a-mist *(Nigella damascena)* follows its blue, pink, or white flowers with inflated, round capsules striped in green and maroon. Breadseed poppies *(Papaver somniferum)* produce ribbed pods of golden beige with a flat scalloped top. The shiny eggplant-colored pods of hyacinth bean *(Dolichos lablab)* are as pretty as the lavender pink blossoms they follow. And the very reason for growing Chinese lantern *(Physalis alkakengi)* is its luminescent dangling lights. Honesty or silver dollar plant *(Lunaria annua)* proves its worth in two seasons. The white or deep pink flowers of late spring give way to flat ovals the size of a silver dollar. Rub

The flowers of Aster frikartii *surround the seeds of blackberry lily* (Belamcanda chinensis), *which appear to be made of polished onyx.*

the brown casing between your fingers (or wait for the wind to do it) to reveal the shiny, translucent parchment beneath.

Early-blooming perennials that have been allowed to go to seed may now be picked. Clematis make feathered whirls; a stem of several whirls adds an interesting texture to fall arrangements. Blackberry lily *(Belamcanda chinensis)* produces yellow or orange-and-yellow striped stars in summer, but it puts on its best show in autumn. The seedpods unfurl to reveal the shiny berries, as pretty as polished black pearls. *Iris foetidus* makes a similar revelation with scarlet berries in a pale gold case. The seed heads of giant yellow knapweed *(Centaurea macrocephela)* look like small artichokes. Speaking of which, both dried artichokes and related cardoons make stunning accents to dried arrangements or displayed in a bowl by themselves.

Many daisy-type flowers have striking seedpods. The dark brown heads of purple coneflower *(Echinacea purpurea)* look like tiny hedgehogs. Those of black-eyed Susan (*Rudbeckia* spp.) resemble brown suede gumdrops.

Pods from the Milkweed family, such as these of Asclepias tuberosa, *have great architectural interest in autumn arrangements.*

Cattails also wear suede coats. You don't see cattails much anymore in fashionable shops, but they have a nostalgic appeal. People used to coat them with hair spray to keep the skins from splitting to unleash the cottony seeds inside. This always spelled "fire hazard" to me; I'd prefer to throw them out when they split. I doubt a coating of styling gel would work.

Two fall favorites of flower arrangers are yucca (*Yucca* spp.) and milkweed *(Asclepias speciosa)*. Each yucca pod has three barrel-shaped, ribbed chambers. The rough texture of the brown and tan exterior contrasts with the smooth, shiny interior when the pods split open to reveal the dark seeds. The pods are clustered a dozen or more, depending on the species, atop thick, straight stems. Milkweed pods are of a more graceful shape, almost like an inflated paisley. Their prickly exterior "shells" often split in half, releasing the silky white plumes that serve to float the dark oval seeds on the autumn breeze. If milkweed pods are picked before they mature and split, they usually don't unleash a flurry of seeds inside the house.

Common roadside weeds that we would never consider allowing inside a proper cutting garden may also be picked for the interesting shapes and textures of their seeds and pods. Alleys or vacant lots might provide a source for dock, burdock, Queen Anne's lace *(Daucus carota),* prickly poppy *(Argemone platycerus),* tumbleweeds, and other wild critters. Ask first, of course, before picking on private property.

AUTUMN PERENNIAL FLOWERS

Late-blooming perennials also provide arrangement material at this time of year. The daisies of autumn are as varied and lovely as those of the summer months. Asters come in lovely shades of white, pink, red, blue, and purple. There are hundreds of cultivars ranging from shorter, cushion types such as 'Purple Dome' or violet-red 'Professor Kippenburg' to tall varieties such as deep pink 'Alma Potschke.' *Aster horizontalis* is an interesting species with tiny pale pink flower clusters along its spreading, architectural stems. They make charming additions to bouquets. *Aster frikartii* blooms a gorgeous shade of blue.

Boltonia asteroides looks much like an aster. 'Snowbank' is a great, late-blooming cultivar with blankets of pure white flowers with small yellow centers. Although it can grow to five or six feet in height or more, Boltonia rarely needs staking. Towering way above it, however, is 'Maximillion' sunflower *(Helianthus maximilliani).* If you can reach high enough to cut its single, golden yellow daisies atop stems up to 12 feet high, they make long-lasting cut flowers. It's easier to pick Helen's flower *(Helenium autumnale).* The plants usually grow 3 to 5 feet tall in yellow, golden yellow, burnt orange, rusty brown, or combinations of several of these colors. The single flowers have brown button centers.

Mums are the flower arranger's best friends in the last part of the season.

They come in an amazing variety of colors and shapes and last an exceedingly long time in water. Some are fully double flowers—the traditional cushion mums in white, yellow, orange, peach, red, and burnt orange—while others are single, daisy-type flowers. Some of the best garden plants in the latter category are pink 'Clara Curtis', peach 'Mary Stoker', and warm pink 'Sheffield Pink'. The most extravagant are the fancy quilled and spoon types from the Orient, as well as the giant "football" mums that used to adorn the dress of every homecoming queen. These specialty mums are usually most successful for commercial greenhouse growers, but there's no reason a home gardening enthusiast can't give them a whirl. They need staking and disbudding (removing all but the center flower as they bud to produce the largest flower), and wind and rain may get the better of their heavy heads.

Goldenrods (*Solidago* spp.) are also part of the daisy family. Their tiny flowers, clustered tightly along their arching stems, tend to disguise their daisy heritage. Some people in the eastern part of the country hold little affection for these common wildflowers, but they still make great cut flowers and add that nostalgic autumn grace to any bouquet. They are especially pretty with contrasting purple or blue asters. By crossing goldenrod with aster, hybridists created a new genus called *Solidaster*. Its flowers are like a larger form of goldenrod—still clinging along the branching stems—in a pleasing shade of butter yellow.

While most of the daisy family grows best in full sun, other late-blooming perennials perform well in partial shade as well. Bugbane *(Cimicifuga)* has an unattractive name but has graceful, ivory-white flowers on long, wiry stems. *C. ramosa* has fuzzy flowers arranged like a bottlebrush, while *C. simplex* has round buttons arranged in rows along the flower spike that open into fuzzy flowers in late autumn.

Obedient plant *(Physostegia virginiana)* produces spikes of flowers similar to snapdragons in pink or white. They have a unique hinge where the flower connects with the stem, allowing the flower arranger to point the "obedient" flowers in any direction. Turtlehead *(Chelone obliqua)* also offers unique flowers in pink or white with an interesting shape like a baby turtle that's just popped his head out of his shell. Another unusually shaped blossom belongs to the toad lily (*Tricyrtus hirta* and *T. formosana*). Supposedly looking like toads sitting on water lily pads (to a gardener with a very vivid imagination), the spotted flowers are nonetheless very attractive and bloom in white, pink, plum, yellow, and green. Toad lilies flourish in moist, shady sites.

Fall in the cutting garden is filled with the bounty of goldenrod, asters, and Maximillian sunflowers.

Sedum spectabile has become an essential part of the flower garden in almost all parts of the country. It thrives in sun or partial shade and stays in bloom for months. 'Autumn Joy' is perhaps the most popular cultivar, with pink flower heads eventually turning to brick red. The blossoms of 'Carmen' and 'Indian Chief' open a brighter reddish pink and also finish with a rusty cast.

The pink or white blossoms of Japanese anemone *(Anemone × hybrida)* look more like spring flowers than fall bloomers. Velvety gray balls of buds open to reveal lustrous petals surrounding a pale green center. The flowers are borne abundantly on stiff, branching stems growing from 2 to 4 feet high.

The recent interest in ornamental grasses has opened up new avenues of exploration for arrangers and designers. Both the blades and the seed heads can

The springlike charm of Japanese anemone comes as a surprise in the autumn cutting garden.

be cut and used effectively. The blades add important vertical accents, while the heads have interesting textures.

Late arrangements benefit from the bounty of the harvest season. Fruit such as apples, plums, and crabapples can be displayed still clinging to their branches in wild fall bouquets or picked and combined with autumn flowers. The same goes for vegetables. Sprays of cherry tomatoes look great dripping from an autumnal arrangement. Squash, pumpkins, and gourds make a holiday party special arranged on tables, mantles, or around the door. The entire home landscape can serve as a source of fresh arranging ideas. Colorful autumn leaves combine dramatically with the berries of fire thorn (*Pyracantha* spp.), holly (*Ilex* spp.), mountain-ash *(Sorbus aucuparia)*, and beautyberry (*Callicarpa* spp.).

Selected Grasses for Cutting

- **Animated oat grass** *(Avena sterilis)*
  Annual with pendent bristly heads that age to tan; don't hang upside down.

- **Blue oat grass** *(Helictotrichon sempervirens)*
  Bluish blades make interesting linear components in bouquets; tawny seed heads are small but attractive; seeds can dry on plants or be hung upside down.

- **Cloud grass** *(Agrostis nebulosa)*
  Annual grass with a light, hazy look; tiny white flowers on foot-tall stems.

- **Maiden grass** *(Miscanthus sinensis)*
  Both blades and seed heads are useful when fresh, tan seed heads are a bit fragile when dry; don't hang upside down to dry.

- **Northern sea oats** *(Chasmanthium latifolium)*
  Flat seed heads dangle from fine threadlike filaments; they age from green to beige; don't hang upside down to dry.

- **Purple fountain grass** (*Pennisetum setaceum* 'Rubrum')
  Both maroon blades and copper and purple-tinged seed heads are useful in fresh and dried arrangements.

Sea oats
(Chasmanthium)

- **Quaking grass** *(Briza maxima, B. minor)*
  Annual grasses with flat, pendent seed heads that dangle from thin filaments; seeds fade to tan and brown; don't hang upside down.

- **Rabbit-tail grass** *(Lagurus ovatus)*
  Tight woolly tufts like cotton (or rabbit tails) on slender stems up to two feet tall; hang upside down to dry.

- **Ruby grass** *(Tricholaena rosea)*
  Annual grass with highly ornamental pyramidal clusters of flowers that age from wine red to purple; dry upright for graceful curved stems or hang upside down for straight stems.

- **Squirrel tail grass** *(Hordeum jubatum)*
  Annual grass with fluffy seed heads that resemble their namesake; cut when seeds are fully "fluffed" and hang upside down.

BERRIES, VEGETABLES, AND FRUIT

- **Apple** (*Malus* spp.)
  Cut a branch or two with ripening apples for a mouthwatering bouquet.

- **Beautyberry** (*Callicarpa* spp.)
  Gorgeous rose-lavender berries are best used fresh; strip off foliage where necessary; berries don't dry well.

- **Bittersweet** *(Celastrus orbiculatus)*
  When the seeds turn orange in their golden husks, cut long stems and weave into arrangements or wreaths.

- **Blackberry lily** *(Belamcanda chinensis)*
  Tan pods burst open into three sections, revealing shiny black berries like polished onyx; long stems are a plus, and berries dry well.

- **Chinese lantern** *(Physalis alkekengi)*
  Dangling miniature lantern globes may be used fresh or dried; don't hang upside down or the lanterns won't dangle correctly.

- **Citrus**
  Cut branches or use single fruits, which can be painted with egg whites and then frosted with sugar; lovely for holiday arrangements.

- **Corn** *(Zea mays)*
  So-called Indian corn is a popular fall vegetable for arrangement; tiny dark red strawberry corn is ideal for wreaths.

Citrus

- **Cotoneaster** (*Cotoneaster* spp.)
  Sprays of orange or red berries with rounded green leaves make good background "fans" for flowers.

- **Crabapple** (*Malus* spp.)
  Cut entire branches for charming additions to large-scale arrangements.

- **Fire thorn** (*Pyracantha* spp.)
  Cut long branches studded with clusters of brilliant orange berries for stunning effects.

- **Gourds**
  Unique patterns and color combinations make gourds a favorite for Thanksgiving in bowls and mantle decorations.

- **Grape holly** (*Mahonia* spp.)
  Dark blue berries in tight clusters have attractive waxy blue sheen like grapes.

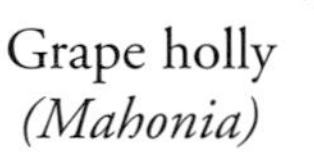

Grape holly *(Mahonia)*

- **Grapes** (*Vinus* spp.)
  Home-grown grapes, either green or purple, look wonderful in cornucopia-style arrangements.

- **Holly** (*Ilex* spp.)
  Scarlet berries are best used fresh, as they shrivel and drop when dried.

- **Juniper** (*Juniperus* spp.)
  Blue cast on the dark berries is highlighted by silvery green foliage; the scent is a plus in holiday bouquets and wreaths.

- **Lily-of-the-valley** *(Convallaria majalis)*
  Best known for its fragrant flowers, but reddish orange fruits about the size of peas are also useful for small bouquets.

- **Lords and ladies** *(Arum italicum)*
  Bright orange berries stud stiff leafless stems; don't dry well.

- **Mountain-ash** *(Sorbus aucuparia)*
  Cut branches with clusters of brilliant orange berries; berries don't dry well.

- **Pear** (*Pyrus* spp.)
  Use branches of fruit or single fruits before they ripen.

- **Pomegranate** *(Punica granatum)*
  Leathery red fruit can be used fresh or dried; dried pomegranates fade to dusty red and are attractive in wreaths and low arrangements.

- **Porcelain vine** *(Ampelopsis brevipedunculata)*
  Lovely blue berries seem appropriate for jewelry; use fresh with stems trailing from bouquets.

- **Pumpkins** *(Cucurbita pepo)*
  From the immense to the miniature, pumpkins spell "autumn" and are at home with other vegetables and cut flowers.

- **Rose** (*Rosa* spp.)
  Cut branches of hips in autumn for fiery red punctuation points in arrangements; hips keep color well when dried.

- **Snowberry** *(Symphoricarpos albus)*
  Puffed little berries don't last long after cutting but add charm to fresh bouquets.

- **Squash** (*Cucurbita* spp.)
  Decorate with them before you eat them.

- **Stinking iris** *(Iris foetidus)*
  Seed capsules open to expose shiny black pearls embedded in the tan shell.

- **Tomatillo** *(Physalis ixocarpa)*
  Often used for cooking, but the inflated pods are cute in arrangements; use fresh when they're green.

An autumnal arrangement of squash, gourds, miniature pumpkins, apples, pinecones, branches, and seedpods looks appropriate in a wooden bowl.

PODS AND SEED HEADS

- **Acorn** (*Quercus* spp.)
  Clusters of nuts are irresistible in autumn projects.

- **Angel's trumpets** *(Datura metel)*
  Prickly round spheres age from blue green to tan; useful in wreaths.

- **Artichoke** *(Cynara scolymus)*
  Easy to dry to a soft olive-tan color; great for wreaths or can be glued to sticks to use in arrangements.

- **Black-eyed Susan** *(Rudbeckia hirta)*
  Felty black gumdrops hold their color; dry on plants — no need to hang and dry.

- **Breadseed poppy** *(Papaver somniferum)*
  Pale green pods are vase-shaped and have scalloped top plate; pods age to golden brown.

- **Canna** (*Canna* spp.)
  Spiky reddish little balls are best used fresh, since they crumble later.

- **Castor bean** *(Ricinus communis)*
  Spiked little balls are best used fresh; they become fragile when dried.

- **Catalpa** *(Catalpa bignonioides)*
  Long, twisted beans have mahogany-like finish.

- **Cattails** *(Typha latifolia)*
  Perhaps a bit overused in the past but still valued for their hot-dog-on-a-stick appeal and soft brown coat.

- **Clematis** (*Clematis* spp.)
  Fluffy seeds need to be handled carefully to keep from shattering; keep arrangement away from breeze.

- **Cones** (pine, spruce, larch)
  Most cones make good accents on wreaths and autumnal bowls of fruit and vegetables.

- **Giant yellow knapweed** *(Centaurea macrocephela)*
  Seed heads are like small, tan artichokes; long stems are an asset.

- **Golden-rain tree** *(Koelreuteria paniculata)*
  Inflated pendent pods have iridescent shades of copper over tan base; pods age well.

- **Honesty** *(Lunaria annua)*
  Rub the dull tan casings between thumb and forefinger to reveal shiny, translucent silver dollars.

- **Honey locust** *(Gleditsia triacanthos)*
  Handle with care to preserve the dark, leathery finish.

- **Hyacinth bean** *(Dolichos lablab)*
  Shiny purple-red pods fade with age and split to release seeds.

- **Lotus** *(Nelumbo nucifera)*
  Large pods resemble upright showerheads; great for wreaths.

- **Love-in-a-mist** *(Nigella damascena)*
  Inflated olive-green pods sport purple-brown stripes; use in short bouquets or wreaths.

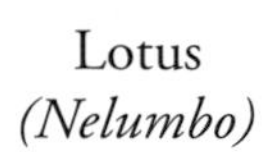

Lotus
(Nelumbo)

- **Magnolia** *(Magnolia grandiflora)*
  Brown overlapping "petals" on seed cones have woody texture.

- **Maple** (*Acer* spp.)
  Cut a whole branch of the two-winged seeds as they take on autumn colors to use as the centerpiece of an autumn grouping.

- **Milkweed** *(Asclepias speciosa)*
  Prickly pods open to reveal smooth golden interior; highly architectural.

- **Purple coneflower** *(Echinacea purpurea)*
  Prickly hedgehog seed heads stay dark brown; long stems are a plus.

Sweet gum
(Liquidambar)

- **Sweet gum** *(Liquidambar styraciflua)*
  Spiked balls resemble tiny medieval maces; use in wreaths and shallow arrangements.

- **Teasel** *(Dipsacus fullonum)*
  A weedy menace if not supervised, but the prickly cones dry to a pleasing brown shade or can be sprayed.

- **Unicorn plant** *(Martynia proboscidea)*
  Slender, pointed pods split when dry into two curved forks.

- **Yucca** (*Yucca* spp.)
  Wood-textured pods are held on long, straight stems; very dramatic in rustic arrangements.

Stars of the cutting gardens include black-eyed Susan, purple coneflower, and yarrow. Yarrow is easy to dry, while the brown cones of black-eyed Susan and coneflower are useful even after the petals drop.

CHAPTER 6
CUTTING AND ARRANGING

Conventional wisdom holds that the best time to cut flowers is in the morning. While this may be true, I think the best time to cut flowers is when you've got the time. I can't always get out in the garden when the roses are still covered with dew. People have showers to take, pets to feed, kids to get off to school, and carpools to catch. High noon is probably not the best time for harvesting fresh flowers—especially if the thermometer is inching into the '90s—but do it when you can. If you need something pretty for a spontaneous get-together, by all means go ahead and take it.

The reason for cutting in the morning is that the stems and leaves will have a high moisture content. So will flower petals, meaning fragrance will be at its peak before the heat of the day causes evaporation and dissipation of the scent. When you cut the stems of most flowers and foliage, immediately set them into slightly cool or tepid water. For best results, use a deep pail or bucket, plunging flowers up to their necks. Singe the ends of flowers with hollow stems, such as poppies and dahlias, with a match to seal the ends. This keeps the moisture in the walls of the stem and helps to keep the hollow tubes from collapsing. Some people get away without this treatment by getting the cut stems immediately into water. Poppies and dahlias most often get the searing flame treatment, but mem-

A freshly picked bouquet includes larkspur, statice, white allium, variegated ivy, and red-twig dogwood.

bers of the mallow family, such as pink mallow *(Malva alcea),* hollyhock *(Alcea rosea),* and striped mallow *(Malva sylvestris,* syn. *Malva zebrina),* also benefit from it. Mallows are usually short-lived in bouquets, but they're spectacular while they last. Individual flowers of problematical plants are sometimes best displayed floating in water, which helps them last a little longer.

Flowers that "faint" after cutting can often be revived by recutting their stems underwater. I run tepid water in the kitchen sink. Holding the stem beneath the surface, I slice off at least an inch of stem with a sharp paring knife. This opens up the freshly cut stem to a drink of water. Roses are often treated this way before they are placed in an arrangement, although florists sometimes cheat by wiring their heads to stay upright. A rose with a nodding head is hard to revive, but you may be able to salvage the situation by cutting the stem very short and nestling it in a short, small vase or, once again, floating it in water. Why do you think they invented the "rose bowl"? It comes in handy.

Some arrangers prefer to condition their cut flowers by keeping them in a cool, dark, humid place for a day. Florists use a refrigerated cooler, which few of us at home have access to. Make do with a basement, closet, or garage. This period of conditioning helps the blossoms and stems to soak up plenty of water to keep them in prime shape for as long as possible once arranged.

That assumes you have time to wait. I'm often guilty of making a spontaneous bouquet: I cut flowers with my pruners and toss them in piles or in a basket if I've remembered one, dump the mess on the kitchen counter, and go at it. This is not an ideal approach, but when company's coming in 20 minutes, it's the only way. A bouquet made like this will be perfectly fine for several days, depending, of course, on what's in it. Cut flowers are not created equal. Some last for weeks and weeks, while others fade after a few days. (If they fade after a few hours, they were not meant for picking.)

How much stem to take when cutting depends on the flower. If you cut a tulip, for example, cut all the way down to the base of the stem, but avoid taking foliage if you want the bulb to produce another flower next year. When cutting lilies, take a minimal amount of foliage for the same reason. Hybrid tea roses are usually cut with several leaves attached; leave about a quarter inch of stem above the uppermost remaining leaf joint. This is where a new bud will

Branches of lemon yellow forsythia, complemented by matching Asiatic lilies, light up a room in late winter.

"break." Shrub roses are usually cut in clusters; new growth will sprout from the last remaining leaf joint.

Most mature shrubs and trees can take quite a bit of "pruning." I try to keep my pickings balanced so the plant doesn't become misshapen. Woody plants need a different type of conditioning. The bottom two or three inches of the cut branch are mashed to allow more water to penetrate the cambium layer (just beneath the bark) and travel upward. I use a metal meat tenderizer when I cut lilacs, forsythias, or apple blossoms, while others prefer a wooden mallet or hammer. The point is not to pulverize the branches to smithereens, but to open up lots of cracks where water can be absorbed.

Most annuals and perennials can be cut on a case-by-case basis, taking as much stem as foliage as needed. Some flowers are positioned in clusters at the top of the stem, such as those of helenium; some are studded along a spike, like delphinium; and many are held singly on a stem, such as scabiosa. It never hurts to cut the whole stem, but consider how much foliage you need, since most of it ends up in a pile on the kitchen counter anyway. When cutting woody plants for their leaves, such as holly or junipers, keep appraising your progress so that the shrub doesn't appear gouged when you're finished.

Not all flowers last for the same length of time in water. Mums, liatris, and alstroemeria last for weeks. Pansies, poppies, and bearded iris last for only a few days. It's all up to the standards of the arranger as to what fits their criteria for a good cut flower. Some flowers shed as they age. I don't find this objectionable in the least, but some people do. They'll pay good money to have petals strewn down a church aisle for a wedding but object when flowers do it voluntarily. Tidy people should be aware that phlox, most salvias, many grasses, and fruit trees and other flowering branches like lilacs and forsythia drop their blossoms. It's either charming or messy, depending on your point of view. Lilies, as mentioned, shed their pollen; some people take scissors and remove the pollen sacks. This detracts from the beauty of the flower—at least to my eyes—and I'd never consider it. On the other hand, I'd never place a bouquet of lilies on my grandmother's lace tablecloth either.

Several strategies can prolong the life of any bouquet. The obvious first step is change the water every day or two. This keeps the buildup of bacteria and molds to a minimum. Some people add a dash of vinegar, a lump of aquarium charcoal, or a few drops of bleach to the water for the same purpose; I've also

Liatris is one of the few flowers that open from the top of the stem downward; a single stem may last several weeks in water.

heard of pennies being tossed into the water, although I'm unaware of copper's ability to keep bacterial growth down. Various recipes for cut flower preservation have been handed down through the generations using all sorts of household products. Not having experimented with them myself, I can't speak for their effectiveness. On the other hand, find out if your aunt, cousin, or neighbor who has a knack for arranging has a secret recipe. It's well worth trying.

I usually stick to clean water, but I sometimes use floral preservative sold at flower shops. You mix this powder, which contains various sugars and starches as well as antibacterials, into tepid water before placing flowers in the vase. If you use floral foam, mix the preservative into the water that the foam soaks in. When using marbles or pebbles for stem support in a container, add the preservative to the water before arranging. It goes without saying that all containers and things such as frogs (metal or plastic holders that sit in the base of a container to anchor stems), marbles, and stones should be washed thoroughly between uses. A dishwasher usually kills most bacteria to keep the slime production down in your vase.

CHAPTER 7
ENDLESS SUMMER

Summer doesn't have to end at the first frost for the flower arranger. When the fresh flowers are gone from the cutting garden, you can begin to harvest everlasting and dried flowers safely tucked in the attic, basement, garage, or barn. Many enthusiasts of everlasting and dried flowers pass the winter months making bouquets that last and last.

Everlasting flowers are those unusual blossoms that look the same when they're blooming as when they've been picked. Strawflowers are the best known of this type. Their many rows of overlapping petals appear to have been cut from parchment paper and have the sheen of straw. The outer petals (properly called bracts) are brightly colored in red, orange, purple, rose, salmon, white, or yellow, shading to ivory near the center of the flower. Picked in their prime—before all the inner petals have opened—the flowers stay exactly as they were at that moment (except for some fading and dust-gathering after too long in the house).

Winged everlasting is named for the raised ridges or "wings" on its stems, which are topped by flowers with silver-white petals and large yellow centers.

An arrangement of everlasting flowers includes strawflowers, globe amaranth, allium, and artichoke, complemented by lotus pods and grasses.

Strawflower is the quintessential flower for drying, since it retains its bright color almost indefinitely.

Swan River everlasting has double daisy flowers up to 3 inches across in white and shades of pink. Immortelle also produces single or double daisylike blossoms with an appealing texture like paper. The flowers are about half the size of those of Swan River everlasting and come in shades of rose, pink, and purple as well as white.

Globe amaranth is a favorite for dried arrangements because of its lovely flower heads that resemble those of clover. A single plant produces an abundance of flowers in lavender, white, pink, scarlet, or magenta. Notched statice *(Limonium sinuatum)* is also popular for its clusters of flowers that appear to have been crafted from colored tissue paper. The colors range from lavender, purple, rose, and blue to white. Algerian statice *(L. bonduellii)* is similar but flowers in yellow. Russian statice *(L. suworowii)* is sometimes called rat-tail statice because of its thin spires of tiny lavender-pink flowers. It's much prettier than the name implies.

Everlasting flowers are extremely easy to cut and dry. Timing is important; cut them at their peak before the colors begin to fade and before the centers of the daisy types start to enlarge. Hang them upside down from a clothesline or wooden drying rack (like one used for clothing). A cool, dry, dark place is best. After just a week or so the flowers may be used in arrangements. The dried stems may be brittle; some arrangers reinforce them with thin wire.

Many garden flowers may be dried successfully and made into arrangements. Some dry almost as easily as everlasting flowers. Lavender (*Lavandula* spp.), yarrow, sea holly, and bear's breeches (*Acanthus* spp.) can be cut and hung to dry and end up looking much like they did before. Other flowers wrinkle up a bit but hold together well. They may lose color and fade to amber and brown, but to many arrangers that's part of the beauty. Roses, larkspur, peonies, and hydrangea look great this way. Hundreds of garden flowers may be dried in this manner, mostly with good results, although some flowers become too fragile and shatter easily.

Some people dry flowers in sand or silica that draws the moisture from petals and leaves. This keeps the flowers from shriveling and keeps the colors brighter. Use a shoe box and gradually "bury" the flowers gently in the sand. It can take several weeks for them to dry completely; unearth them gently and brush away sand with a feather. A different, but classic way of preserving flowers is with a flower press or heavy encyclopedia. This is perfect for flat-faced flowers like pansies. Many people enjoy making cards and pictures from pressed flowers.

EVERLASTING FLOWERS

- **Baby's breath** *(Gypsophila paniculata)*
  Easy perennial with white or pink single or double tiny flowers produced in airy profusion.

- **Balloon vine** *(Cardiospermum halicacabum)*
  Vine with puffed seedpods 1 inch in diameter, fading from green to tan.

- **Chinese lantern** *(Physalis alkekengi)*
  Inflated orange globes deserve their common name; cut before they burst open; color fades somewhat.

- **Cockscomb** *(Celosia cristata)*
  Striking flower heads bear a resemblance to rooster combs in red, orange, or yellow; colors fade slowly with age.

- **German statice** *(Goniolimon tataricum)*
  Perennial with masses of tiny lavender-blue flowers on brown stems; hang to dry just as flowers open.

- **Globe amaranth** *(Gomphrena globosa)*
  Easy annuals that revel in heat; cut when heads first open and colors will stay brilliant.

- **Immortelle** *(Xeranthemum annuum)*
  Color stays fresh if cut and hung to dry just as flowers open.

- **Job's tears** *(Coix lacryma-jobi)*
  Hard-shelled seeds in white, gray, brown, or black in clusters on graceful curved stems; dry upright to preserve stem curvature.

- **Statice** (*Limonium* spp.)
  Colors hold remarkably true if harvested at their peak.

- **Strawflower** *(Helichrysum bracteatum)*
  Cut before the center petals of each flower open; colors hold extremely well; hang upside down to dry.

- **Swan River everlasting** *(Helipterum manglesii)*
  Harvest when flowers first open to hold color; hang upside down.

- **Winged everlasting** *(Ammobium alatum)*
  Winged stems are nearly as important as the white flowers; hang separately rather than in clusters.

The steely blue flowers of sea holly (Eryngium planum) *are set off by the silver foliage of Artemisia 'Valerie Finnis' in the garden as well as in bouquets.*

FLOWERS FOR DRYING

- **Acanthus** (*Acanthus* spp.)
  Let dry on plant before picking; very interesting sepals stud upright stems.

- **Bells of Ireland** *(Molucella laevis)*
  Hang upside down to dry; green color holds well.

- **Cotton**
  The pods open to expose fluffy white balls; don't need to be hung; use full stem or detach balls for wreaths.

- **Globe thistle** *(Echinops ritro)*
  Steely blue color resists fading if picked early; hang upside down for best results.

- **Hydrangea** (*Hydrangea* spp.)
  Colors fade somewhat or take on green or brown tones; hang upside down to dry and handle carefully.

Hydrangea
(Hydrangea)

- **Jerusalem sage** (*Phlomis* spp.)
  Not necessary to hang but helpful to preserve straight stems with tiers; flowers fade to tan.

- **Joe-Pye weed** *(Eupatorium purpureum)*
  Mauve tones of large flower heads fade a bit; hang upside down to dry and handle carefully.

Joe-Pye weed
(Eupatorium)

- **Larkspur** *(Consolida ambigua)*
  Hang upside down; colors hold up best
  in pastel shades.

- **Mealy-cup sage** *(Salvia farinacea)*
  Hang upside down to dry; color holds fairly well.

- **Peony** (*Paeonia* spp.)
  Hang upside down; handle carefully when dry; colors fade but still have
  charm.

- **Pussy willow** (*Salix* spp.)
  Dries easily; can be used fresh and then again after drying.

- **Roses** (*Rosa* spp.)
  Hang upside down to dry; colors fade to pleasing "Victorian" shades.

- **Sea holly** (*Eryngium* spp.)
  Silver color best preserved if cut just as flowers open,
  hang upside down to dry.

- **Showy stonecrop** *(Sedum spectabile)*
  Not necessary to hang upside down; flowers turn brown and brick red.

- **Yarrow** *(Achillea coronaria, A. millefolium)*
  Best if dried upside down but not absolutely necessary;
  gold *A. coronaria* holds its color fairly well.

- **Zinnia** *(Zinnia elegans)*
  Hang upside down to dry;
  bright colors fade but pastels stay best.

Yarrow
(Achillea)

The brick pink flower heads of Sedum 'Autumn Joy' are easily dried.

INDEX

Page numbers in italics refer to illustrations or photographs.

Abyssinian gladiolus, 75–76
Acanthus spp., 109, 112
Acer spp., 98
Achillea
  coronaria, 68, 113
  millefolium, 68, 113
  ptarmica, 68
  tagetya 'Anthea', 68
  tagetya 'Moonshine', 68
Acidanthera, sweet-smelling, 3
Acidanthera bicolor. See Gladiolus callicanthus
Aconitum spp., 67, 74
Acorn, 96
African marigold, 51, *82,* 84
Agapanthus
  'Storm Cloud', 75
  common blue, 75
Agapanthus, 74–75
Ageratum
  houstonianum, 51
  houstonianum 'Cut Wonder', 49
Ageratum 'Cut Wonder', 51
Agrostis nebulosa, 91
Alcea rosea, 102
Alchemilla vulgaris, 12, 68
Algerian statice, 108–9
Allium
  drumstick, 74
  as everlasting flower, *106*
  as spring bulb, 38
  as summer flower, *54*
  white, *100*
Allium
  aflatunense, 74
  caeruleum, 14, 74
  cristophii, 74
  giganteum, 74
  moly, 38, 40
  ostrowskianum, 38, 40
Allspice, Carolina, 63
Almond, 32
Alstroemeria, 104
Alstroemeria, 74–75
Amaranth, globe, 3, *106,* 108, 110
Amaryllis, 42
Ammi majus, 51
Ammobium alatum, 110
Ampelopsis brevipedunculata, 16, 94
Anemone
  Japanese, 89, *90*
  for West Coast or South, 42
Anemone
  coronaria, 42
  × *hybrida,* 89
Anemone-type dahlia, 76
Angel's trumpets, 96
Animated oat grass, 91
Annual baby's breath, 27
Annuals
  for autumn bouquets, *82,* 83–84
  cool-season, 18, 44–45
  high-altitude, *57,* 58–61
  planting of, 27
  shade-tolerant, 55–56
  for summer bouquets, *48,* 49–55
Anthemis, 67
Antirrhinum majus, 45, 61
Apple
  in autumn bouquets, 91, 92, *95*
  cutting of, 104
  in spring bouquets, 3, 31, 32
Apricot, 32
Aquilegia spp., 74
Argemone platyceras, 87
Arrangements. *See also* Autumn bouquets; Spring bouquets; Summer bouquets
  in autumn, 83–99
  branches in, 12, 31–34
  care of, 4, 101–4
  foliage in, 3
  and garden design, 12–14, 17–18
  longevity of, 104–5
  in spring, 31–47
  in summer, 49–81
Artemisia
  'Valerie Finnis', *111*
  and garden design, 14
  silver, *6*
Artemisia spp., 14
Artichoke, 85, 96, *106*
Arum italicum, 94
Aruncus dioicus, 14, *18,* 67, 74
Asclepias
  speciosa, 86, 87, 98
  tuberosa, 86
Ash, 31
Asiatic lily
  'Apollo', 79
  'Ariadne', 79
  'Brushstroke', 79
  'Cherry Smash', 79
  'Chianti', 79
  'Citronella', 79
  'Doeskin', 79
  'Fireworks', 79
  'Flirt', 79
  'Hornpipe', 79
  'Joanna', 79
  'Kiss Me Kate', 80
  'Last Dance', 79
  'My Fair Lady', 80
  'Plum Crazy', 79
  'Red Velvet', 79
  'Royal Dream', 80
  'Royal Highness', 80
  'Royal Perfume', 80
  'Tiger Babies', 79
  'Tinkerbell', 79
  'Yellow Blaze', 79
  in arrangements, 14, *103*
Aspen, 31, 32
Aster
  as autumn flower, 3, *89*
  china, 52
  planting of, 27
Aster
  frikartii, 85, 87
  horizontalis, 87
Astilbe spp., 74
Astrantia spp., 74
Aurelian. *See* Trumpet lily
Aurinia saxitilis, 46
Autumn bouquets
annuals for, *82,* 83–84
berries for, 3, 92–94
fruit and vegetables for, 17, 91
ornamental grasses for, 14, 89–92
perennials for, 87–89
seedpods for, 4, 14, 84–87, *95,* 96–99
Autumn perennials, 87–91
Avena sterilis, 91
Babiana stricta, 42
Baboon flower, 42
Baby gladiolus, *77*
Baby's breath, *17*
  annual, 27
  perennial, 12, 67, 109
Bachelor's button, 3, *6,* 27, 51, 70
Balloon vine, 109
Balsam, 27, 49, 51
Basil, Chinese, 14
Basket-of-gold, 46
Bean
  castor, 96
  hyacinth, 16, 84, 97
  scarlet runner, 11
  as warm-season crop, 10
Bearded iris, 40, 41, 104
Bear's breeches, 109
Beautyberry, 91, 92
Beauty bush, 63
Beds, design within, 8–12
Bee balm, 67
Begonia, wax, 56
Begonia semperflorens, 56
Belamcanda chinensis, 14, *85,* 92
Bellflower
  milky, 70
  peach-leaf, 12–14, 70
  as summer perennial, 70
Bellis perennis, 44
Bells of Ireland, 112
Bergenia cordifolia, 46, 47
Berries, 3, 17, 92–94
Betula spp., 32
Biennials, 55–56, 72
Birch, 31, 32
Bishop's weed, 51
Bittersweet, 16, 92
Blackberry lily, 14, *85,* 92
Black-eyed Susan, *vi–1*
  as annual, 49, 52, 58, 84
  in autumn bouquets, 3, 12, 14, 96, *99*
  as perennial, 67
  seedpods of, 85
Blazing star, 78
Bleeding-heart, 46, 47
Blossoms, shedding of, 104
Blue lace flower, 14, 49, 52
Blue oat grass, 91
Blue ornamental onion, 14

Boltonia asteroides, 87
Boltonia 'Snowbank', 87
Bouquets. *See* Arrangements; Autumn bouquets; Spring bouquets; Summer bouquets
Branches, 12, 31–34, *95*
Brassica oleracea, 44
Breadseed poppy, 84, 96
Bridal veil, 3
Briza
maxima, 92
minor, 92
Brodiaea, 38, 40
Bronze fennel, 14
Brown-eyed Susan, 72
Buddleia
'Nanho White', *64*
alternifolia, 63
davidii, 63
Bugbane, 88
Bugler, scarlet, 67
Bulbs
for spring bouquets, *30,* 31, 35–43
for summer bouquets, 74–78
for West Coast or South, 42
Burdock, 87
Burgundy pincushion flower, 70
Buttercup, Persian, 42, *43*
Butterfly bush, 63, *64,* 75

Cactus-flowered dahlia, 76
Cactus-flowered zinnia, 50
Caladium
'White Queen', 55
× *hortolanum,* 55
Calendula officinalis, 18, *19,* 45, 61
Calla lily, 42
Callicarpa spp., 91, 92
Callistephus chinensis, 52
Calycanthus floridus, 63
Camassia, 38, 40
Camassia
leichtlinii, 40
quamash, 40
Campanula
lactifolia, 70
latifolia, 70
medium, 72
persicifolia, 12–14, 70
punctata, 70
rotundifolia, 70
Campsis radicans, 16
Candelabra primrose, 46
Candytuft, 55
Canna spp., 96
Canterbury bell, 72
Cardinal flower, 74
Cardiospermum halicacabum, 109
Cardoon, 85
Care of cut flowers, 101–4
Carolina allspice, 63
Caryopteris
incana, 63
× *clandonensis,* 63
Castor bean, 96
Catalpa bignonioides, 96
Catananche caerulea, 67
Catmint
'Six Hills Giant', 68
'Walker's Low', 68
Cattail, 86, 96
Ceanothus spp., 63
Celastrus orbiculatus, 16, 92
Celosia cristata, 110
Centaurea
cyanus, 27, 51
dealbata, 70
macrocephala, 70
macrocephela, 85, 97
montana, 70
Cephelaria
alpina, 70
gigantea, 70
Cercis
canadensis, 34
species, 34
Chaenomeles spp., 32
Chamaebatiaria millefolium, 64
Chasamanthium latifolium, 14, 91
Chasmanthe spp., 42
Cheiranthus cheiri, 45
Chelone obliqua, 88
Cherry, 31, 32
Cherry, sand, 14
Cherry tomato, 12, 91
China aster, 52
Chinese basil, 14
Chinese coral lily, 79
Chinese lantern, 16, 84, 92, 110
Chionodoxa luciliae, 40
Chrysanthemum
'Clara Curtis', 88
'Mary Stoker', 88
'Sheffield Pink', 88
in arrangements, 14, 104
as autumn flower, 3
as perennial, 87–88
types of, 88
Cimicifuga
ramosa, 88
simplex, 88
Citrus, 32, 93
Clarkia elegans, 45, 61
Clematis, 16, *17,* 85, 97
Clematis spp., 16, 97
Cleome, *71. See also* Spider flower
Cleome hasslerana, 27, *28,* 52, 84
Clethra
anifolia, 63
species, 63
Climbing hydrangea, 16
Climbing rose, *62*
'Blaze', 63
'Maiden's Blush', 63
'New Dawn', 63
Cloud grass, 91
Cockscomb, 110
Coix lacryma-jobi, 110
Coleus, 49, 52, 55
Coleus blumei, 52, 55
Color, 14, *19*
Columbine, 3, 74
Common blue agapanthus, 75
Coneflower, purple, *6,* 67, 85, 98, *99*
Cones, 97
Conifers, 4
Consolida ambigua, 27, 113
Convallaria majalis, 38, 40, 93
Cool-season plants, 18, 44–45
Coralbells, 68
Coreopsis, *10*
Coreopsis spp., 3, *4,* 67
Corn, 12, 18, 93
Corylus avellana 'Contorta', 34
Cosmos
as annual, 49, 52, *53*
as autumn bloomer, *82*
direct seeding of, 27
and garden design, *6, 10*
Cosmos bipinnatus, 27, 52
Cotinus coggygria, 14
Cotoneaster spp., 93
Cottage pink, 72
Cotton, 112
Cotton lavender, 14
Crabapple, 31, 91, 93
Creeper, Virginia, 16
Crinum lily, 42
Crinum × *powelli,* 42
Crocosmia
masonorum 'Lucifer', 76
× *crocosmiflora,* 76
Cucubita spp., 16
Cucurbita
pepo, 94
species, 94
Cupid's dart, 67
Curly willow, 31, 32
Cushion-type chrysanthemum, 88
Cutting and arranging
care of flowers when, 101–4
longevity after, 104–5
Cutting garden
autumn flowers for, *82,* 83–99
cutting and arranging from, 100–105
design of, 6–19
dried flowers from, *111,* 112–15
everlasting flowers for, *106,* 107–10
introduction to, 3–5
maintenance of, 23–28, *29*
planning of, *20,* 21–22
reasons for growing, 1–2
spring flowers for, *30,* 31–47
summer flowers for, *48,* 49–81
Cynarascolymus, 96

Daffodil
'Accent', 36
'Actea', 37
'Carlton', 36
'Cassata', 36
'Ceylon', 36
'Geranium', 36
'Golden Ducat', 36
'Ice Follies', 36
'Jenny', 36
'King Alfred', 36
'Minnow', 36
'Mount Hood', 36
'Orange Progress', 36
'Palmares', 36
'Pheasant's Eye', 37
'Rip van Winkle', 36
'Salome', 36

'Scarlet O'Hara', 36
'Silver Chimes', 36
'Sundial', 36
'Tête-à-tête', 36
'Thalia', *35,* 36
'White Lion', 36
and garden design, 12, 14
as spring flower, 3, 36, 40
Peruvian, 78
Dahlia
'Babylon Bronze', 76
'Bishop of Llandaff', 76
'Ellen Houston', 76
'Firebird', 76
'Flowerfield', 76
'Jean Marie', 76
'Kelvin Floodlight', 76
'Lavender Perfection', 76
'Park Princess', 76
'Promise', 76
'Thomas A. Edison', 76
as autumn annual, 83, 84
as climber, 8
as summer bulb, *71,* 76–78
care of, 28, 77–78, 101–2
scarlet, 14
types of, 76
Dahlia-flowered zinnia, 50
Daisy
'Alma Potschke', 87
'Professor Kippenburg', 87
'Purple Dome', 87
English, 44
and garden design, *9, 13,* 14, 18
gloriosa (*See* Black-eyed Susan)
painted, 67
as perennial, 87
Shasta, *11,* 67
snow, 67
Daisy-flowered zinnia, 50
Daisy-type chrysanthemum, 88
Daphne
odorata, 32
species, 32
Darwin hybrid tulip, 38
Datura metel, 96
Daucus carota, 56, 84, 87
Delphinium
care of, 28, *29*
cutting and arranging of, 14, 104
and garden design, 8, *17*
as summer perennial, 67
Design
within beds, 8–12
with color, 14, *19*
and foliage, 14–17
and garden design, *6,* 7–8, 12–14, 18
and and garden design, 16
and site selection, 7–8, 22
Dianthus, 44
Dianthus
× *allwoodii,* 72
× *allwoodii* 'Daphne', 72
× *allwoodii* 'Helen', 72
× *allwoodii* 'Ian', 72
× *allwoodii* 'Robin', 72
barbatus, 69, 72
chinensis, 61
deltoides, 72
plumarius, 72
Dicentra spectabilis, 46
Dictamnus albus, 28
Digitalis purpurea, 56, 72
Dinner plate dahlia, 76
Dipsacus fullonum, 90
Dock, 87
Dogwood, red-twig, 4, *100*
Dolichos lablab, 16, 84, 97
Doronicum caucasicum, 46
Dried flowers, *111,* 112–15
Drumstick allium, 74
Drying, 112–15
Dusty miller, 14, 27, 44, 58
Dutch iris, 40, 41

Early perennials, 46–47
Echinacea purpurea, 67, 85, 98
Echinops ritro, 14, 70, 112
Elder, 64
Enclosures, *6,* 7–8
English daisy, 44
English primrose, 46–47
Eryngium
planum, 14
species, 28, 70, 113
Eucomis punctata, 78
Euonymus, 17
Eupatorium purpureum, 112
Everlasting
Swan River, 107–8, 110
winged, 107, 110
Everlasting flowers, *106,* 107–10

Fall. *See* Autumn bouquets; Autumn perennials
False sunflower, 67
Fennel, bronze, 14
Fernbush, 64
Fertilizing, 22–23
Feverfew
and garden design, *9*
golden-leafed, 14
as summer perennial, 67
Filbert, 31
Filipendula
species, 74
ulmaria, 68
venusta 'Rubra', 68
Fire thorn, 91, 93
Flame flower, 42
Flax, New Zealand, 14
Floribunda rose, 62–63
Flowering quince, 32
Flowering tobacco
'Domino', 84
'Starship', 84
as cool-season annual, 44, 84
and garden design, *5*
as high-altitude annual, 58
planting of, 27
as summer annual, 49
Flowers
cut, care of, 101–4
cut, longevity of, 104–5
dried, *111,* 112–15
everlasting, *106,* 107–10
Foeniculum vulgare 'Purpureum', 14
Foliage, *3,* 14–17
"Football" chrysanthemum, 88
Forget-me-not, 44, 72
Forsythia
cutting of, 104
lemon yellow, *103*
in spring bouquets, 3, 12, 31, 34
Forsythia spp., 34
Fountain grass, *20*
purple, 91
Foxglove
'Foxy', 56
as biennial, 72
as shade-tolerant, 56
in summer bouquet, *54, 62*
Freesia, 42
Freesia × *hybrida,* 42
French marigold
'Lemon Gem', 84
'Tangerine Gem', 84
Fritillaria persica, 38, 40
Fruit, 12, 17, 91, 92–94, 104. *See also* individual fruits
Gaillardia aristata, 3, *5,* 67
Galanthus nivalis, 40
Galium vernum, 68
Garden phlox, *vi–1*
'Amethyst', 70
'Brilliant Eye', 70
'David', 70
'Mt. Fuji', 70
Garland, Rocky Mountain, 45, 61
Gas plant, 28
Gayfeather, Kansas, 78
German statice, 110
Giant pincushion flower, 70
Giant yellow knapweed, 85, 97
Gladiolus, *vi–1*
Abyssinian, 75–76
baby, *77*
nanus, 75, *77*
as summer flower, 3
Gladiolus
byzantinus, 75
callicanthus, 75–76
Gleditsia triacanthos, 97
Globe amaranth, 3, *106,* 108, 110
Globe thistle, *9,* 14, 70, 112
Gloriosa daisy. *See* Black-eyed Susan; *Rudbeckia hirta*
Glory-of-the-snow, 3, 31, 40
Glossy holly, 4
Goatsbeard, 14, *18, 54,* 67, 74
Godetia amoena, 45, 61
Golden hops vine, 14
Golden-leafed feverfew, 14
Golden-rain tree, 97
Goldenrod, 88, *89*
Gomphrena globosa, 3, 110
Goniolimon tataricum, 110
Gourd, 3, 16, 91, 93, *95*
Grape, 16, 93
Grape holly, 93
Grape hyacinth, 40
Grass. *See also* Ornamental grass
animated oat, 91
blossom shedding of, 104
blue oat, 91
as everlasting flower, *106*
fountain, *20*
with gladiolus, 75
maiden, *15,* 91
Gum, sweet, 98
Gypsophila
elegans, 27
paniculata, 67, 109

Hamamelis spp., 34
Harebell, 70
Harlequin flower, 42
Harry Lauder's walking stick, 34
Heder helix, 16
Helenium, 104
Helenium autumnale, 67, 87
Helen's flower, 67, 87
Helianthus
  annuus, 55
  maximilliani, 87
Helichrysum bracteatum, 3, 110
Helictotrichon sempervirens, 91
Heliopsis spp., 67
Heliotrope, 56
Heliotropium arborescens, 56
Helipterum manglesii, 110
Hellebore, 31
Helleborus
  orientalis, 47
  species, 46
Herbs. *See* individual herbs
Hesperis matronalis, 72
Heuchera, 68
High-altitude annuals, *57,* 58–61
Hip, rose, 4
Hippeastrum × *hybridum,* 42
Holly
  in arrangements, 17, 93
  berries of, 91
  cutting of, 104
  glossy, 4
  grape, 93
  sea, 14, 28, 70, 109, *111,* 113
Hollyhock, 102
Honesty, 56, 58, 84–85, 97
Honey locust, 97
Honeysuckle, 16, *54*
Hops, 16
Hops vine, golden, 14
Hordeum jubatum, 92
Hosta
  'Aphrodite', 74
  and garden design, 14
Hosta plantaginea, 74
Humulus lupus
'Aureus', 14, 16
'Variegatus', 16
Hyacinth
'Blue Jacket', *2*
  grape, 40
  as spring bulb, 3, 36, 40
  wood, 38, *39,* 40
Hyacinth bean, 16, 84, 97
Hyacinthoides hispanica, 38, *39,* 40
Hyacinthus spp., 40
Hybrid polyantha primrose, 46
Hybrid tea rose
  'Double Delight', 62
  'Mr. Lincoln', 62
  'Peace', 62
  cutting of, 102
  and garden design, 18
Hydrangea
  climbing, 16
  drying of, 109, 112
Hydrangea
  petiolaris, 16
  quercifolia, 112
  species, 112
Hymenocallis aestivus, 78

Iberis umbellata, 55
Iceland poppy, *25,* 44, *57,* 58
Ilex spp., 91, 93
Immortelle, 108, 110
Impatiens balsamina, 27, 49, 51
Indian blanket, 3, *5,* 67
Indoor arrangements, 12–14
Iris
  bearded, 40, 41, 104
  Dutch, 40, 41
  Siberian, 40, 41
  Spanish, 40, 41
  as spring bulb, 3, 40
  spuria, 40, 41, *54*
  stinking, 94
Iris
  foetidus, 85, 94
  germanica, 40
  sibirica, 40
  spuria, 40
  xiphioides, 40
  × *hollandica,* 40
Ivy, 16, *100*

Japanese anemone, 89, *90*
Jasmine, 16
Jasminum spp., 16
Jerusalem sage, 112
Job's tears, 110
Joe-Pye weed, 112
Juniper, 93, 104
Juniperus spp., 93

Kale, ornamental, 44, 45
Kansas gayfeather, 78
Knapweed, giant yellow, 85, 97
Knautia macedonica, 70
Kniphofia uvaria, 67
Koelreuteria paniculata, 97
Kolkwitzia amabilis, 63

Lace, Queen Anne's, 56, 84, 87
Lace flower, blue, 14, 49, 52
Lady's bedstraw, 68–70
Lady's mantle, 12, 68–70
Lagurus ovatus, 92
Landscape rose
  'Ferdy', 63
  'The Fairy', 63
Lantana, *48*
Larch, 97
Larkspur
  in arrangements, 14, *100*
  direct seeding of, 27, 49
  drying of, 109, 113
  and garden design, *10*
Lathyrus
latifolius, 16
  odoratus, 16, 45, 61
Lavandula spp., 109
Lavender
  cotton, 14
  drying of, 109
  and garden design, 14
Lemon yellow forsythia, *103*
Lenten rose, 46, *47*
Leopard's bane, 46, 47
Leucojum vernum, 38, 40
Liatris, 3, 104, *105*
Liatris, 78
Lilac, 3, 34, 104
Lilium
  candidum, 79, *81*
  hansonii, 79
  martagon, 79
  pumilum, 79
Lily
  Asiatic, 14, 79–80, *103*
  blackberry, 14, *85,* 92
  calla, 42
  Chinese coral, 79
  crinum, 42
  and garden design, 12, 14, *17*
  Madonna, 79, *81*
  martagon, 79
  Oriental, 80–81
  Peruvian, 74
  pineapple, 78
  pollen shedding of, 104
  spider, 42
  in summer bouquets, 79–81
  toad, 88
  trumpet, 80
Lily-form tulip, *37,* 38, *41*
Lily-of-the-Nile, 74
Lily-of-the-valley, 2, 38, 40, 93
Limonium
  bonduellii, 108–9
  sinuatum, 108
  species, 110
  suworowii, 109
Liquidambar styraciflua, 98
Lobelia cardinalis, 74
Locust, honey, 97
Longevity of cut flowers, 104–5
Lonicera
  japonica, 16
  species, 16
Lords and ladies, 94
Lotus, 97, *106*
Love-in-a-mist
  as annual, 49, 58
  in autumn bouquets, 97
  direct seeding of, 27
  seedpods of, 84
  as shade-tolerant, 56
Lunaria annua, 56, 58, 84–85, 97
Lungwort, 46
Lupine, 67
Lupinus, 67
Lycoris radiata, 42

Macleaya cordata, 68
Madonna, 79, *81*
Magnolia
  grandiflora, 34, 97
  species, 34
Mahonia
  nevinii, 93
  species, 93
Maiden grass, *15,* 91
Maiden pink, 72
Maintenance
  fertilizing, 22–23
  sowing seeds, 3, 23–24
  staking plants, 28, *29*
  transplanting, 24–28
  watering, 22
Mallow
  care of, 101–2
  pink, 102
  striped, 102

Malus
pumila, 32
species, 92, 93
Malva
alcea, 102
sylvestris syn. *Malva zebrina,* 102
Maple, 31, 98
Marigold, *vi–1*
African, 51, *82,* 84
as annual, 18
French, 84
planting of, 23, 27
pot, 18, *19,* 45, 61
signet, 84
Martagon, 79
Martynia proboscidea, 98
Masterwort, 74
Matthiola incana, 18, 45, 61
'Maximillion' sunflower, 87, *89*
Meadow rue, *54,* 67–68
Meadowsweet, 68, 74
Mealy-cup sage, *48,* 49, 52, 84, 113
Meidiland series rose, 63
Mexican hat, 67
Mexican sunflower, 52, 83
Milkweed, 86, 87, 98
Milky bellflower, 70
Mina lobata, 16
Miniature pumpkin, *95*
Miscanthus sinensis, 91
Mock orange, 3, 64
Molucella laevis, 112
Monarda didyma, 67
Monkshood, 67, 74
Montbretia, 76
Morning glory, 11
Mountain-ash, 91, 94
Muscari armeniacum, 40
Myosotis
sylvatica, 44
sylvestris, 72

Nanus gladiolus, 75, 77
Narcissus spp., 40
Nelumbo
lutea, 97
nucifera, 97
Nemesia strumosa, 44, 58
Nepeta sibirica, 68
Nerine bowdenii, 42
New Zealand flax, 14
Nicotiana
alata, 27, 44, 58, 84
sylvestris, 49, 56, *64,* 84
Nicotiana 'Salmon Pink', *26*
Nigella damascena
direct seeding of, 27
seedpods of, 58, 84, 97
as shade-tolerant, 56
as summer annual, 49
Northern sea oats, 14, 91
Notched statice, 108

Oat grass
animated, 91
blue, 91
Oats, northern sea, 14, 91
Obedient plant, 88
Oleander, 65
Olearia spp., 65
Onion
blue ornamental, 14
ornamental, 40, 74
Opium poppy, 27
Orange, mock, 3, 64
Orchid, poor man's, 45, 61
Oregano, 14
Oriental lily
'Allura', 80
'Bessie', 80
'Black Beauty', 81
'Casablance', 80
'Coral Bee', 80
'Harbor Star', 80
'Imperial Gold', 80
'Journey's End', 80, 81
'Lemon Meringue', 80
'Marco Polo', 80
'Oregon Mist', 80
'Pink Ribbons', 80
'Red Jamboree', 80
'Salmon Jewels', 80
'Sans Souci', 80
'Stargazer', 81
'Sweet Frost', 80
'Tickled Pink', 80
"rubrum", 81
Ornamental grass
animated oat, 91
in autumn bouquets, 89–92
blue oat, 91
cloud, 91
as everlasting flower, 3
fountain, *20*
and garden design, 14
maiden, *15,* 91
northern sea oats, 14, 91
purple fountain, 91
quaking, 92
rabbit-tail, 92
ruby, 92
squirrel tail, 92
striped Hakonechloa macra, *15*
as summer flower, *62*
Ornamental kale, 44, 45
Ornamental onion
blue, 14
as spring bulb, 40
as summer bulb, 74

Paeonia spp., 113
Painted daisy, 67
Painted tongue, 59
Pansy
as cool-season annual, 44, 45
drying of, 109
in high-altitude garden, *57,* 59
longevity of, 104
as shade-tolerant, 56
Papaver
nudicaule, 44, 58
rhoeas, 27, 45, 61
somniferum, 27, 84, 96
Parthenocissus tricuspidata, 16
Partial-shade perennials, 74
Passiflora spp., 16
Passionflower, 16
Pea
as cool-season crop, 18
perennial, 16
sweet, 2, 8, 11, 16, 45, 49, 61
Peach, 31, 34
Peach-leaf bellflower, 70
Pear, 31, 34, 94
Pennisetum setaceum 'Rubrum', 91
Penstemon
Rocky Mountain, 67
shell-leaf, 67, *69*
in summer garden, *62*
Penstemon
barbatus, 67
palmeri, 67, *69*
strictus, 67
Peony
'Bowl of Beauty', 65, *66*
'Crinkled White', 65
'Festiva Maxima', 65
'Nippon Beauty', 65
'Primevere', 65
'Sarah Bernhardt', 65
'Seashell', 65
drying of, 109, 113
and garden design, 12, 18
as spring flower, 3
in summer bouquets, 65–66
tree, 66
Perennial baby's breath, 12
Perennial pea, 16
Perennials
for autumn bouquets, 87–91
for partial shade, 74
shade-tolerant, 55–56
for spring bouquets, 46–47
for summer bouquets, 67–74
Perilla frutescens, 14, *26*
Perovskia atriplicifolia, 68
Persian bells, 38, 40
Persian buttercup, 42, *43*
Peruvian daffodil 'Sulfur Queen', 78
Peruvian lily, 74
Philadelphus spp., 64
Phlomis spp., 112
Phlox
blossom shedding of, 104
garden, *vi–1,* 70
with gladiolus, 75
as summer perennial, *71*
Phlox paniculata, 70
Phormium spp., 14
Physalis
alkakengi, 84
alkekengi, 16, 110
ixocarpa, 94
Physostegia virginiana, 88
Pieris japonica, 35
Pincushion flower
as annual, 49, 59, 84
burgundy, 70
as extended bloomer, 3
giant, 70
as perennial, 70
Pineapple lily, 78
Pinecones, *95,* 97
Pink
cottage, 72
in high-altitude garden, *57,* 61
maiden, 72
mallow, 102
as perennial, *69*
Planning
and plant selection, *20,* 21
and site selection, 7–8, 22

- Plants
  - fertilization of, 22–23
  - selection of, *20,* 21
  - shade-tolerant, 55–56
  - staking of, 28, *29*
  - transplanting of, 24–28
  - watering of, 22
- Plum, 31, 34, 91
- Plume poppy, 68
- Pods, 3, 17, 96–99
- Polyantha primrose, hybrid, 46
- *Polyanthes tuberosa,* 78
- *Polygonatum odoratum,* 38, 40
- *Polygonum aubertii,* 16
- Pomegranate, 94
- Poor man's orchid, 45, 61
- Poppy
  - breadseed, 84, 96
  - care of, 101–2
- Iceland, *25,* 44, *57,* 58
- longevity of, 104
- opium, 27
- plume, 68
- prickly, 87
- Shirley, *19,* 27, 45, 49, 61
- sowing of, *25*
- *Populus tremula,* 32
- Porcelain vine, 16, 94
- *Potentilla* spp., 65
- Pot marigold, 18, *19,* 45, 61
- Powder puff dahlia, 76
- Prickly poppy, 87
- Primrose
  - candelabra, 46
  - English, 46–47
  - hybrid polyantha, 46
  - as spring flower, 3, 46
- *Primula*
  - species, 46
  - *veris,* 46–47
- Privet, 17
- *Prunus*
  - *armeniaca,* 32
  - *cistena,* 14
  - *dulcis,* 32
  - *persica,* 34
  - species, 32, 34
- *Pulmonaria* spp., 46
- Pumpkin
  - in arrangements, 3
  - in autumn bouquets, 91, 94, 95
  - in autumn garden, *82*
  - miniature, *95*
- *Punica granatum,* 94
- Purple coneflower, *6,* 67, 85, 98, *99*
- Purple fountain grass, 91
- Purple-leafed smoke bush, 14
- Pussy willow, 31, 34, 113
- *Pyracantha* spp., 91, 93
- *Pyrethrum* spp., 67
- *Pyrus* spp., 34, 94

- Quaking grass, 92
- Queen Anne's lace, 56, 84, 87
- Queen-of-the-meadow, 68
- *Quercus* spp., 96
- Quilled-type chrysanthemum, 88
- Quince
  - flowering, 32
  - and garden design, 12
  - in spring bouquets, 3, 31

- Rabbit-tail grass, 92
- Radish, 18
- Raised beds, 8–11
- *Ranunculus asiaticus,* 42, *43*
- *Ratibida columnifera,* 67
- Rat-tail statice, 109
- Redbud, 34
- Red-hot poker
  - 'Primrose Beauty', 67
  - and garden design, 14
- Red-twig dogwood, 4, *100*
- *Ricinus communis,* 96
- Rocket, sweet, 72
- Rocky Mountain garland, 45, 61
- Rocky Mountain penstemon, 67
- *Rosa*
  - *alba,* 63
  - species, 94, 113
- Rose
  - 'Austrian Copper', 63
  - 'Harrison's Yellow', 63
  - 'Persian Yellow', 63
  - in arrangements, 12, 14, 94
  - climbing, 8, *62,* 63
  - drying of, 109, 113
  - fertilizing of, 23
  - floribunda, 62–63
  - hip, 4, 12
  - hybrid tea, 18, 62, 102
  - landscape, 63
  - lenten, 46, *47*
  - Meidiland series, 63
  - rugosa, 63
  - shrub, 18, 62–63, 104
  - in summer bouquets, 62–63
- Ruby grass, 92
- *Rudbeckia*
  - *hirta,* 3, 52, 58, 84, 96
  - species, 67, 85
  - *triloba,* 72
- Rue, meadow, *54,* 67–68
- Rugosa rose 'Therese Bugnet', 63
- Russian sage, 68
- Russian statice, 109

- Sage
  - Jerusalem, 112
  - mealy-cup, *48,* 49, 52, 84, 113
  - Russian, 68
- *Salix*
  - *chaenomeloides,* 34
  - *sachalinensis* 'Sekka', 32
  - species, 113
- *Salpiglosis sinuata,* 58
- Salvia, 52, *54,* 55, 104
- *Salvia*
  - *farinacea, 48,* 49, 52, 84, 113
  - *nemorosa,* 68
  - *splendens,* 55
  - *verticillata,* 68
- *Sambucus*
  - *caerulea,* 64
  - *canadensis,* 64
- Sand cherry, 14, 31
- *Santolina chamaecyparissus,* 14
- Satin flower, 45, 61
- Scabiosa, 104
- *Scabiosa*
  - *atropurpurea,* 59, 84
  - *caucasica,* 70
  - species, 3
- Scarlet bugler, 67
- Scarlet dahlia, 14
- Scarlet runner bean, 11
- *Schizanthus wisetonensis,* 45, 61
- *Scilla sibirica,* 40
- Sea holly
  - drying of, 109, 113
  - as everlasting flower, *111*
  - and garden design, 14
- as perennial, 70
- propagation of, 28
- Sea oats, northern, 14, 91
- Sedum
  - 'Autumn Joy', 89, *114*
  - 'Carmen', 89
  - 'Indian Chief', 89
- *Sedum spectabile,* 89, 113
- Seed heads, 96–99
- Seedpods, 3–4, 17, 84–87, *95,* 96–99
- Seeds
  - sowing of, 3, 23–24
- Selection
  - of plants, *20,* 21
  - of site, 7–8, 22
- *Senecio cineraria,* 14, 44, 58
- Shade-tolerant plants, 55–56
- Shasta daisy, *11,* 67
- Shell-leaf penstemon, 67, *69*
- Shirley poppy, *19,* 27, 45, 49, 61
- Showy stonecrop, 113
- Shrub rose, 18, 62–63, 104
- Shrubs, 63–65
- Siberian iris, 40, 41
- Signet marigold. *See* French marigold
- Silver artemisia, *6*
- Silver dollar plant. *See* Honesty
- Silver-lace vine, 16
- Site selection, 7–8, 22
- Smoke bush, purple-leafed, 14
- Snapdragon, 27, 45, 49, *60,* 61
- Snowberry, 94
- Snow daisy, 67
- Snowdrop, 31, 40
- Snowflake, summer, 38, 40
- Soil, 22
- *Solidago* spp., 88
- *Solidaster,* 88
- Solomon's seal, 38, 40
- Sorbus, 65
- *Sorbus*
  - *aucuparia,* 91, 94
  - species, 65
- Sowing seeds, 3, 23–24
- Space and design, 18
- Spanish iris, 40, 41
- *Sparaxis tricolor,* 42
- Spider flower, 27, *28,* 52, 84. *See also* Cleome
- Spider lily, 42
- Spinach, 18
- Spirea, 65
- *Spirea*
  - *japonica, 65*
  - species, 65
- Spoon-type chrysanthemum, 88

Spring bouquets
  branches for, 12, 31–34, *95*
  bulbs for, *30,* 31, 35–43
  cool-season annuals for, 18, 44–45
  perennials for, 46–47
Spruce cones, 97
Spuria iris, 40, 41, *54*
Squash, 3, 18, 91, 94, *95*
Squill, 31, 40
Squirrel tail grass, 92
Staking plants, 28, *29*
Statice
  Algerian, 108–9
  in bouquets, *100*
  as everlasting flower, 110
  and garden design, *10*
  German, 110
  notched, 108
  rat-tail, 109
  Russian, 109
Stinking iris, 93
Stock, 18, 45, 61
Stonecrop, showy, 113
Strawflower, 3, *106,* 107, *108,* 110
Striped Hakonechloa macra, *15*
Striped mallow, 102
Summer bouquets
  annuals for, *48,* 49–55
  biennials for, 72
  bulbs for, 74–78
  high-altitude annuals for, *57,* 58–61
  lilies for, 79–81
  partial-shade perennials for, 74
  peonies for, 65–66
  perennials for, 67–74
  roses for, 62–63
  shade-tolerant plants for, 55–56
  shrubs for, 63–65
Summer snowflake, 38, 40
Sunflower
  'Maximillion', 87, *89*
  as autumn flower, *82*
  false, 67
  and garden design, *6*
  Mexican, 52, 83
  as warm-season annual, 3, 18, 49, 55
Susan, black-eyed, *vi–1*
  as annual, 49, 52, 58, 84
  in autumn bouquets, 3, 12, 14, 96, *99*
  as perennial, 67
  seedpods of, *85*
  brown-eyed, 72
Swan River everlasting, 107–8, 110
Sweet gum, 98
Sweet pea
  as annual, 45, 49, 61
  and garden design, 8, 11
  as vine, 16
Sweet rocket, 72
Sweet-smelling acidanthera, 3
Sweet William, *9,* 72, *73*
Symphoricarpos albus, 94
Syringa spp., 34

Tagetes erecta, 51
Tall verbena, 49, 55
Tanacetum
  niveum, 67
  parthenium, 67
  parthenium 'Aureum', 14
Teasel, 98
Thalictrum aquilegifolium, 67–68
Thistle, globe, *9,* 14, 70, 112
Tickseed, 3, *4,* 67
Tithonia rotundifolia, 52, 83
Toad lily, 88
Tobacco
  flowering, *5,* 27, 44, 49, 58, 84
  woodland, 49, 56, 84
Tomatillo, 94
Tomato, cherry, 12
Tongue, painted, 59
Torenia fournieri, 56
Trachymene caerulea, 14, 49, 52
Transplanting, 24–28
Tree and shrub branches, 12, 31–34, *95*
Tree peony, 66
Tricholaena rosea, 92
Tricyrtus
  formosana, 88
  hirta, 88
Triteleia laxa, 38, 40
Tritonia crocata, 42
Trumpet lily
  'Black Dragon', 80
  'Copper King', 80
  'Golden Sceptre', 80
  'Lady Anne', 80
  'Midnight', 80
  'Summer Palace', 80
  'White Henryi', 80
Trumpet vine, 16
Tuberosa 'The Pearl', 78
Tuberoses, 3
Tulip
  'Angelique', 38, *41*
  'Apledoorn', 38
  'Apricot Beauty', 38
  'Attila', 38
  'Ballerina', 38
  'Elegant Lady', 38
  'Elizabeth Arden', 38
  'Hans Anrud', *30*
  'Jewel of Spring', 38
  'Mariette', 38
  'Orange Sun', *2*
  'Queen of the Night', 38
  'Triumphator', 38
  'West Point', 38
  'Yellow Apledoorn', 38
  Darwin hybrids, 38
  and garden design, 12, 18
  lily-form, *37,* 38, *41*
  as spring bulb, 3, 36, 40
Tulipa spp., 40
Tumbleweed, 87
Turban flower, 42. *See also* Persian buttercup
Turtlehead, 88
Typha latifolia, 96

Unicorn plant, 98

Variegated ivy, *100*
Vegetables, 18, 91, 92–94. *See also* individual vegetables
Verbena
  as annual, 84
  tall, 49, 55
Verbena
  patagonica, 49, *64*
  patagonica syn. *Verbena bonariensis,* 55
Veronica
  'Crater Lake Blue', 68
  'Icicle', 68
  and garden design, *13,* 68
Veronica spicata, 68
Viburnum
  plicatum var. *tomentosum,* *65*
  species, 65
Vine
  balloon, 109
  golden hops, 14
  list of, 16
  porcelain, 94
Vinus spp., 93
Viola wittrockiana, 44, 56, 59
Virginia creeper, 16
Vitex spp., 16

Wallflower, 44
Warm-season
  annuals, *48,* 49–55
  bulbs, 74–78
  crops, 18
  perennials, 67–74
Watering, 22
Wax begonia, 56
Weeds, 12
Weigelia spp., 65
White allium, *100*
White yarrow, *13*
William, sweet, *9,* 72, *73*
Willow
  curly, 31, 32
  pussy, 31, 34, 113
Winged everlasting, 107, 110
Winterberries, 4
Wishbone flower, 56
Witch hazel, 31, *33,* 34
Wood hyacinth, 38, *39,* 40
Woodland tobacco, 49, 56, 84

Xeranthemum annuum, 110

Yarrow
  'Cerise Queen', 68
  'Lavender Lady', 68
  'Paprika', 68
  'Summer Pastel', 68
  in autumn bouquets, *99*
  drying of, 109, 113
  with gladiolus, 75
  as perennial, *62,* 68
  white, *13*
Yucca spp., 86–87, 98

Zantedeschia aethiopica, 42
Zea mays, 93
Zinnia, *vi–1*
  'California Giant', *50,* 51
  as autumn annual, 84
  as best annual for cutting garden, 50–51
  drying of, 113
  and planning, *20*
  sowing of, 23
  as summer annual, 3, 18, *48,* 49, 55
  types of, 50
Zinnia
  angustifolia, *48,* 51
  elegans, 55, 84, 113
Zucchini, *82*

Titles available in the Taylor's Weekend Gardening Guides series:

Organic Pest and Disease Control
Safe and Easy Lawn Care
Window Boxes
Attracting Birds and Butterflies
Water Gardens
Easy, Practical Pruning
The Winter Garden
Backyard Building Projects
Indoor Gardens
Plants for Problem Places
Soil and Composting
Kitchen Gardens
Garden Paths
Easy Plant Propagation
Small Gardens
Fragrant Gardens
Topiaries & Espaliers
Cold Climate Gardening
The Cutting Garden
Cooking from the Garden

At your bookstore or by calling 1-800-225-3362